PREACHING FROM THE SOUL

PREACHING FROM THE SOUL

INSISTENT OBSERVATIONS ON THE SACRED ART

J. ELLSWORTH KALAS

Abingdon Press
Nashville

Library of Congress Cataloging-in-Publication Data

Kalas, J. Ellsworth, 1923-
    Preaching from the soul / J. Ellsworth Kalas.
    *13*p. cm.
      ISBN 0-687-06630-1 (pbk.)
      1. Preaching. I. Title.

BV4211.3 .K35 2003
251—dc21

16 ⁰⁰   2002153042

03 04 05 06 07 08 09 10 11 12—10 9 8 7 6 5 4 3 2 1

MANUFACTURED IN THE UNITED STATES OF AMERICA

To My Preaching Students

To some, for making me think
I was doing it right

To others, for convincing me
I'd better keep working at it

To all, with love

Contents

Introduction

One summer evening some thirty years ago, my philosophy of preaching found its name. I suspect that my first ideas about the meaning of preaching began finding form when I was not yet eleven years old, and felt that I was called to preach. Probably every evangelist and pastor that I listened to in the next dozen years contributed to this definition in some fashion or other, though neither they nor I knew it. But I didn't have a name for it until that summer evening, in a pleasant eating place not far from Chautauqua, New York.

The conversation was one that picked up regularly on hundreds of summer evenings over many years. I was the senior pastor of the First United Methodist Church in Madison, Wisconsin, a pulpit as fulfilling as any pulpit in America. Brevard "Bard" Childs was professor of Old Testament at Yale University, in both the graduate school and the Divinity School. He was already a distinguished scholar and author of several landmark books in his field, while I was telling myself that I would someday write a book.

That evening, Bard asked if I had a particular idea for a book in mind. I did, but frankly it wasn't very good, and that book—mercifully—has never been written. Then Bard said, "You ought to write a book on preaching. And you know what you should call it? *Soul Preaching.*"

I didn't really know what he meant. In fact I wasn't even sure that he was serious; we treated matters lightly those evenings of lazy, rambling conversations.

But whether he was serious or not, I knew that he had found the word for what I believed about preaching. And from that point on, *soul preaching* became the point around which all of my homiletical inclinations gathered.

What Soul Preaching Is Not

When I speak of soul preaching, I'm not thinking of the role of preaching in saving souls. Of course no preaching is able, of itself, to save souls. The act of redemption is divine business, and preaching simply makes its contribution to that holy enterprise. The task of soul winning, soul nurture, and the growth of the soul is, in my judgment, a given; any preaching that doesn't work to these ends hardly deserves to be called preaching.

Nor am I speaking of soul preaching in the way that an African American preacher might use the term. In truth, I feel it would be presumptuous for me so to use it. I have a feeling, however, that African American preachers may well have better instincts for soul preaching than do persons of my ethnic heritage. And probably their congregations do a better job of encouraging such preaching. But soul preaching is not the singular province of any ethnic or denominational group. Indeed (and here I will upset some), in its essence, soul preaching is not even limited to the ordained or called clergy. I suspect that there was the quality of soul preaching in William Jennings Bryan's "Cross of Gold" speech, and in Franklin Delano Roosevelt's address to the American people after the bombing of Pearl Harbor.

What Soul Preaching Is

Soul preaching happens when the speaker seeks to deliver not only a message, but his or her own soul, and to deliver it in such a way that it reaches the soul of the hearer. The speaker is communicating ideas, insights, and convictions, but all of these are marked by the quality of the speaker's own soul. As a result, soul preaching is intensely personal, because it comes from the soul, the innermost totality of the speaker, with the intention of reaching that same innermost place in the hearer. Such preaching is inherently passionate.

Soul preaching may well make some hearers uneasy. If the hearer prefers to keep a safe distance from the speaker, soul preaching is threatening. On the other hand, this is the only kind of preaching that really matters, because it is the deep calling to the deep. Soul preaching abhors the superficial, whether the issue is intellectual, emotional, or creative. I suppose, logically, that a superficial person can deliver superficial soul, but something about the very concept is somewhat obscene.

Soul preaching pays its listeners the ultimate compliment. It says that the speaker believes so much in the worth of the hearer that he or she risks the baring of the soul. One of my students said, after preaching an especially soul-felt sermon, "I seemed to be stripped naked." Of course. That's just what we do when we truly preach. We dare to let someone into our soul. They come to know us at the depths of life. Mind you, I'm not speaking of the kind of thing popularly known as "letting it all hang out." The pulpit is not customarily a confessional in which we reveal the soap opera of our lives. But it *is* a confessional in the sense that Saint Augustine used the word; it is the place where we confess our faith, and in doing so we become truly and magnificently vulnerable.

Let me offer a caveat here. It is no doubt true that many who listen to a sermon don't warrant such a risk on the part of the preacher. If they come casually, wanting only the accoutrements of religion, wanting only to fulfill some social or civic obligation, they hardly justify the compliment of the preacher's passion. But soul preaching is reckless, because it is so intent on the worth of the message it delivers and on the worth of the person who may receive it. And the soul preacher realizes that, because "the wind bloweth where it listeth," there is no predicting when a casual listener may become a passionate one (John 3:8 KJV).

Soul Preaching's Lineage

Ecclesiastes is right; there's nothing new under the sun. My concept of soul preaching has ancient roots. I'm quite sure that when Jeremiah wanted to escape his call, he found he could not because

> then within me there is
> something like a burning
> fire
> shut up in my bones;
> I am weary with holding it in,
> and I cannot. (Jeremiah 20:9)

When Jeremiah expressed such an experience, he described soul preaching at its most painful. He had delivered his soul to his people, and they rejected it; and in their rejection, Jeremiah—like many of us—concluded that God had rejected him as well.

Isaiah was a soul preacher; what else could he be after the coal from the altar touched his lips? Jonah's problems came because he had soul even when he didn't want one. And Hosea is, of course, the patron saint of all soul preachers.

But they are examples of the art, rather than its definers. I'm quite sure that soul is inferred in Aristotle's classical discussion of rhetoric. You will recall that Aristotle spoke of three forms of persuasion—the rational appeal *(logos)*, the emotional appeal *(pathos)*, and the ethical appeal *(ethos)*. Ethos, in the philosopher's thinking, came from the character of the speaker. He felt that three essential qualities made for such persuasive character—manliness (or what we might now call "inner strength"), kindliness, and wisdom. And while logos and pathos were essential to persuasive speaking, Aristotle felt that ethos was the most powerful of the three. In Aristotle's view, ethos was powerful in persuasion not simply because it resided in the speaker, but because it expressed itself *in the speech itself*.[1] This is an important distinction. Some of the finest and most admirable persons I have ever known have not been particularly effective preachers. And, I regret to say, some effective preachers haven't always struck me as the most admirable people. Indeed, this is one of the anomalies of the public platform, whether sacred or secular, that scoundrels or near-scoundrels are sometimes bewitching at the podium. Their stories surface again and again in the annals of politics, religion, and snake oil sales. The issue is not simply the character of the speaker, but the elements that come through in the speaker's presentation.

Now, this unpleasant fact may not present a problem to the snake oil salesman or the unscrupulous politician, but it does for the preacher. Or, more correctly, it ought to. We stand, not at a speaker's podium, but at the sacred desk. The pulpit is the altar of God. Most of us, at our ordination, received an assignment to "the Word and the sacraments." We perform the sacraments at the altars of the communion table and the baptismal font or baptistry, and we deliver the Word at the altar of the pulpit.

At our best we sense, like Richard Baxter, that we stand between the living and the dead. Our sermons, whether great or fumbling, may be the watershed of eternity. Since this is so, the sermons we deliver must come from as good a soul as grace and our own stringent commitment can deliver. We need have no doubt about the contribution of grace. Commitment, discipline, and integrity depend on us.

We dare not allow ourselves to become cynical if we see persons of questionable motives or methods achieving apparent or real success. Indeed, we would do well to follow Saint Paul's lead. In his imprisonment, he recognized that some were now proclaiming Christ "out of selfish ambition, not sincerely but intending to increase my suffering in my imprisonment." And to that Paul said, with cavalier abandonment, "What does it matter? Just this, that Christ is proclaimed in every way, whether out of false motives or true; and in that I rejoice" (Philippians 1:17-18). At the same time, if you're a spiritual journeyer, you may want to consider two thoughts: perhaps I am judging the other person unfairly, not realizing the virtues that override his or her shortcomings; and also, my business is never really the mote in my brother's or sister's eye, but the beam in my own.

Well over a century ago, an Episcopal rector and bishop, Phillips Brooks, defined preaching in a phrase that remains the most quoted and probably the most succinct. Preaching, he said, is "the communication of truth through personality."[2] The concept of "personality" no doubt has different configurations today than it did when Brooks spoke it in his Beecher Lectures; and as a matter of fact, with deconstructionism somewhat in vogue, the concept of "truth" is also being redefined. But the major insights are the same, and the definition has its kinship with soul preaching.

If preaching means communicating truth through personality, then the filter through which all preaching passes, for better or worse, is the preacher's soul. When I was nineteen years old, and doing a fair bit of preaching, I read that it takes twenty years to make a sermon because it takes twenty years to make a preacher. I realized that the aphorism was true, and that I was therefore working on short supply, but I cherished the hope that perhaps the Holy Spirit would make up the deficit. I now realize that the Spirit is always making up one deficit or another; and that while nothing quite takes the place of time and experience (I speak from the comfortable vantage point of later years), the passage of time does not itself guarantee those qualities in a preacher that make for soul. In fact, sometimes the passage of time seems to diminish soul. The incomprehensible becomes manageable, and the ineffable is rendered commonplace. The teenager once gave a witness that's likely to be soul on Youth Sunday, but as a middle-aged, well-ordained, and somewhat jaded preacher, he or she now delivers platitudes.

As a teacher of preaching, I feel that one of my greatest challenges is to develop the gifts of students without diminishing their souls. I don't want to blur their uniqueness. To the contrary, I want to set it free. Obviously, no students come to me in a virginal state; they've already heard enough sermons that they reflect other souls. And that's as it should be, of course, because all of us are the products not only of our genes, but also of all those persons whose lives intersect with ours. If, as John Donne said, "any man's death diminishes me," it is as surely true that every person's life enriches me.

But the teacher may want to reshape a student's soul. The teacher thinks, "that peculiar gesture: is it an awkwardness I must work to remedy, or a reflection of who this person is? This rather obtuse way of approaching a theme and a text: is it a lack of good education, or a peculiar stroke of genius?" God uses a patrician Isaiah and a spitfire Amos; Jeremiah, a man of peace, dreads challenging the king, while Elijah rejoices in the conflict. The teacher had better leave the students' souls intact, otherwise the kingdom will suffer. However, the teacher had also better deal with their ambiguities and their gaucheries or they will founder in mediocrity.

Call is a very big issue in soul preaching. We go about our audacious task because God has ordained our doing so. Some may question God's judgment and taste in choosing us; at times, we may wonder ourselves. But one thing is sure, God is not displeased by our variety. The God who gives individuality to snowflakes and to infinite varieties of beetles, and who invests each of us with singular voices, fingerprints, and footprints, must surely want those who are called to guard the uniqueness that is invested in them. I am passionate about doctrinal integrity, but I think the worst heresy might be for all of us to recite our beliefs with the same accent.

So there is a particular purpose in the calls you and I have received. It is not that we should become another Billy Graham or another Harry Emerson Fosdick. It is that we should give to God the unique soul that we possess, because with that special soul God can do what cannot be done with any other soul.

I have mentioned only Aristotle and Phillips Brooks in suggesting something of the lineage of soul preaching, but I suspect that the essence of the idea can be found in any number of the finest preachers over the centuries. William Quayle, who was not only a bishop of the Methodist Episcopal Church but also one of the best-known preachers of his day, said that the art of preaching is to make a preacher, and deliver that. That's soul. P. T. Forsyth, who influenced the English speaking world as both theologian and preacher in the early twentieth century, said, "A true sermon is a real deed. It puts the preacher's personality into an act."[3] Harry Emerson Fosdick, probably the best-known pulpiteer in America from 1930 to 1950, said that he tried to "get hold of live issues that really mattered . . . then put it across to people as hot as I can."[4] I call that soul.

The Implications of Soul

To preach with soul means that soul is present in the sermon from conception to delivery. The preacher saturates himself or herself at length in the text before going into commentaries or other material, else the sermon will have the flavor of such sources rather than the flavor of the preacher's beliefs. This is at least part of what the crowds must have meant in Jesus' day when they saw him as teaching "as one having authority, and not as their scribes" (Matthew 7:29). The scribes were superb scholars, but they were all quotes and no blood.

I suspect that the soul preacher will rarely find illustrations in a book of stories or on the Internet, because such sources give little opportunity for the preacher to claim a tie to his or her soul. Soul preaching requires not only that the illustration fit the sermon, but also that it fit the preacher. Mind you, the illustration need not be original with the preacher; it would be an extraordinary person indeed who could claim that every story had been mined by his or her own hand, from novels and biographies, histories and experiences. But the illustrations need to capture the preacher, so that the hearer realizes that they belong to the preacher, like children, either by blood or by adoption; they are not neighbor children dressed up for this Sunday's parade.

The voice, the gestures, the bearing are also the preacher's own. I have great regard for good theater. But the pulpit is not a performance; it is an incarnation. The preacher should learn everything possible about proper use of the voice, so that the people can enjoy it for twenty or thirty minutes at a time, and the preacher can use his or her voice for fifty or sixty years. The pulpit voice should have the quality of personal declaration, not of a practiced professionalism. One should learn enough about gesturing that one seems to be neither a mummy still bound, nor a windmill gone astray; the gestures must also be natural to the preacher. One can learn to gesture for a stage play; I am skeptical about learning gestures for a sermon. The difference? The stage always expects the audience to suspend disbelief, while the pulpit works on precisely the opposite presupposition; our hearers should be compelled to listen with the question, "Is this the truth, and is it being truthfully said?"

The Sum of It All

The goal, in short, is for the preacher to deliver his or her soul to the people. This presupposes that the preacher will have taken proper care of that soul, so there is something worth delivering. To change the figure of speech momentarily, we are the channels through which God delivers the water of life. For that reason, our lives should be as free of unholy "sediment" as possible. We preachers are, after all, sinners saved by grace, so we leave our human smudges on each message we bring. And apparently, God is pleased that it is done this way.

Even so, it's frightening to think that the eternal message, the announcement of a plan that the Apostle said was in God's mind from before creation, should be delivered through messengers of such varied ages, talents, and commitments. The only thing we have fully in common is that none of us is qualified for the task. But we do it by the grace of God, and that's appropriate, since it is grace that we declare.

Whatever our qualifications, one thing is sure: we had better deliver the message with the highest level of excellence of which we are capable. Let me say it again; whether we are male or female, young or old, educated or barely literate, we must be *excellent*. After all, we speak for the Lord of the universe, and the souls to whom we speak are eternal. So we deliver to them *our* soul—the very best of our soul. Nothing less will do.

Notes

1. Edward P. J. Corbett and Robert J. Connors, *Classical Rhetoric for the Modern Student* (New York: Oxford University Press, 1999), 19.

2. Phillips Brooks, *Lectures on Preaching* (New York: E. P. Dutton and Company, 1902), 5.

3. P. T. Forsyth, *Postive Preaching and the Modern Mind*, 2d ed. (Pittsburg: Pickwick Press, 1981), 122.

4. Robert Moats Miller, *Harry Emerson Fosdick: Preacher, Pastor, Prophet* (New York: Oxford University Press, 1985), 342.

CHAPTER ONE

Take the Bible Seriously

No better thing can happen to our preaching than having a passionate love affair with the Bible. This isn't easy for us preachers. We suffer the burden of familiarity, and in most cases (as a seminary professor, I hate to say it), we also suffer the burden of an education. We become too bookish about the Book, so that we see it as a source of sermons and studies, and we are more taken with problems of scholarship than with the wonders of its continuing power. As for familiarity, I suspect that the Hollywood divorce rate indicates that even glamour becomes commonplace unless it is sustained by uncommon love. We need a grand love for the Bible because it is our basic document. It is not only the particular source of our preaching, but it is also the book that so uniquely understands us, that we gain our understanding of life through it.

But of course we twenty-first century preachers have special problems with the Bible. We may sometimes wish that we could read it as if there had never been the explosion of critical studies, but the fact is, we have lost our innocence. Even those who scorn critical studies acknowledge the importance of these studies by their attacks on them. The effective preacher confronts the issues of biblical criticism like a lover who has seen his romance almost scuttled, but who now loves more knowingly and earnestly than before the period of trauma.

One way or another, the preacher must have a unique relationship with the Bible. For me, it is the inspired Word of God. I see it as unlike any other book, in its origin and in its authority. I meet professional colleagues who think my position is a bit strong, but who honor the Bible as the document of the church and its traditions. Still others, it seems to me, haven't necessarily thought through a personal theology of the Scriptures, but they cherish the Bible for what it has meant in their own life and experience. Although I would rather preachers see the Bible as I do, I want them to enter the study and the pulpit with any devotion to the Book that will drive them to search it, clarify it, and deliver it with conviction. To that end, I suggest some practical rules, some of them quite obvious, but not always faithfully practiced.

1. Believe that the Bible is for every reader, now. Protestant clergy love to talk about the priesthood of all believers, and about the open Bible for all God's people, but we tend to take a professional proprietary interest in it. Intentionally or not, we sometimes give people the feeling that they can never hope to understand the Scriptures as well as we do. It's obviously true that we have an academic edge, since we've specialized in biblical studies. It's also quite possible that at an experiential level, the person in the pew may relate to the Bible better than we do. Our professionalism may get in the way. So while we ought to employ everything we know about Greek, Hebrew, ancient history, and Middle Eastern geography, we want to be very careful not to give people the feeling that without such knowledge their own reading is inadequate. Our preaching receives a high compliment when it inspires people to read the Bible for themselves, both studiously and devotionally. Approach preaching with the conviction that the Bible is God's gift to our human race, and that it is, therefore, intended to be understood.

The "now" in this first suggestion is especially significant. I venture that every effective preacher has tried, as it is so often said, to have one foot in the Bible and one foot in the present. If any particular individual ought to have a feeling for the times in which we live, it should be the preacher—particularly the parish pastor. More than the historian, more than the newscaster, more than the political pundit or the social philosopher, the preacher ought to have a feeling for his or her time. We must somehow know the spirit of the age, yet avoid being either captured by it, or cheaply exploiting it.

2. Know the Bible's every jot and tittle, but read it as if you had never seen it before. I suppose this rule seems quite unrealistic. I confess that I'm giving the counsel of perfection, but I'm confident it is within our reach. This is the attitude of love; but those who have loved deeply know that even the best love has to be nurtured. I've read through the Bible in its entirety several dozen times, and expect to do so again next year. I've been helped to see it anew by using different translations from time to time. I've also been helped by seeing the Bible through the eyes of novelists and poets, as in *Congregation: Contemporary Writers Read the Jewish Bible*, edited by David Rosenberg, and its New Testament counterpart, *Incarnation*, edited by Alfred Corn. Indeed, whenever I see Scripture approached by a serious novelist or poet, I look with interest. I don't need to agree with their theology, but I do need the stimulus of their thinking.

I remind myself of the ancient rabbis who insisted that the Torah has seventy faces. I find new wonders as I seek with hunger and openness. I remember, too, John Robinson, pastor to the Plymouth Pilgrims, who assured his flock when they left for the New World that there was still more light to break forth from God's holy Word. If there is any limitation to the inspiration and insight to be found in the Scriptures, it is the limitation we bring by our low expectations. Some years ago a reviewer commented that most productions of plays by J. M. Synge, the brilliant Irish playwright, were "marred by the arid hand of the academicians, who revere a play's reputation as a 'classic' without ever understanding the vital impulse that inspired it."[1] Those of us who teach and preach the Bible may well be guilty of the same marring of the Scriptures, which brings us to the next rule.

3. Be properly skeptical of yourself. Each of us approaches the Bible with our own prejudices. William Blake put the matter humorously, as he noted our inclination to see Christ's image in our own image: "Thine has a great hook nose like thine / Mine has a snub nose like to mine." I take the Scriptures with all seriousness, but I try to be much less serious about my own understanding and interpretation of Scripture. The pastor ought always to preach out of his or her heart; one's preaching ought surely to have soul. But we preachers must also remember that we can too easily fixate on themes that reflect either our prejudices or our struggles, and that we need therefore to come under the discipline of the teachings of the church, perhaps the structures of the lectionary, and the guidance of some insightful, honest friend.

4. Don't be afraid to wrestle with the Scriptures. Frederick Buechner is an ordained Presbyterian minister who has devoted most of his ministry to writing. As a result, he has sat in the pew more frequently than do most of us preachers. He has found it an unsettling experience. He says of the preachers he has heard, "There is precious little in most of their preaching to suggest that they have rejoiced and suffered with the rest of mankind"; "they tend to become *professionals* who have mastered all the techniques of institutional religion and who speak on religious matters with what often seems a maximum of authority and a minimum of vital personal involvement."[2] But Buechner gratefully recalls sermons by "a man named Robert MacFarlane." Those sermons, he said, "had spaces in them, spaces of silence as if he needed those spaces to find deep within himself what he was going to say next, as if he was giving the rest of us space to think for a moment about what he had just been trying to say last." Buechner feels confident that the man was laying out "a faith that, even as he spoke it, he was drawing out of the raw stuff of his own life."[3]

Sermons like MacFarlane's have soul. They are not just scholarly investigations or interesting topics to be explored, but a personal wrestling. Still more, it is not only that the preacher is wrestling with this text because of what the text means in his or her life, but that, as a pastor, there is a wrestling on behalf of all the people. I no longer have the pastoral role, but on those frequent weekends when I am preaching somewhere around the country, I seek to have a pastoral heart. This is a heart that recognizes that everyone is compelled to do a fair share of wrestling—some occasionally, and some through all of their struggling lives. It is part of the preacher's calling to wrestle vicariously on behalf of the people who will eventually hear the Word. Because we spiritually wrestle for others, we examine the Scriptures, then preach them, in a manner that is both dreadfully and wonderfully affirming of existence.

5. Practice psychological exegesis. I'm afraid of this term being misunderstood. By "psychological exegesis," I'm simply urging that, in our reading of the Bible, we seek to get inside the characters. Perhaps this desire is behind my enthusiasm for the insights on Scripture that come from poets, novelists, and playwrights. Paddy Chayefsky gave me insights on Gideon, in his play of the same name, that I didn't find in commentaries, because Chayefsky had looked into Gideon's soul.

I remember, in a sermon about the man whose son would often convulse and foam at the mouth (Luke 9:37-43), a student who gave us a moment to feel the pain of the father, and as he did we were able to feel the father's poignant sorrow and despair as he appealed to Jesus to do for his boy what the disciples had proved unable to do. There were no histrionics; such pain needs no embellishment. The student simply took us inside the father's heart for a moment, and helped the story engage us. In feeling the father's exquisite pain, I entered a whole new dimension in the story of the boy's healing.

The Bible is wonderfully candid about the lives of its characters. It never gives us plaster of paris saints. We need to follow the Bible's lead in examining the fears, frustrations, joys, and displeasures of its personalities. The book of Psalms, by itself, has enough varieties of emotions to occupy a stable of soap opera writers for a decade. Paul's epistles are packed full of doctrine, but Paul's emotions are woven in, through, and around the doctrine. He reasoned with his congregations, but usually with a hot pen; for him, doctrine was always blood and sinew.

I realize that a lazy preacher might take my words as license to push aside research and engage instead in undisciplined imagining. I'm not urging that we fill our sermons with what Paul, David, or Peter "must have felt"; a little of that fare goes a long way. But we do well to invest our souls in the souls of the biblical writers and characters in the hope that we may get new light for the text itself. Scripture passages are rarely, if ever, cold statements of fact; they are stories and convictions born in experience.

Perhaps we sometimes miss the heartbeat of the biblical personalities because we have not ourselves experienced as much as we should of our faith or of life. George Macdonald, the preacher turned novelist, portrays a cleric in his novel *Sir Gibbie*, who "knew nothing whatever but by hearsay," because he "had not in himself experienced one of the joys or one of the horrors he endeavored to embody."[4] Obviously we preachers can't be expected to encounter all the vicissitudes and glories of life, nor can we travel each pilgrim pathway. It may not be inappropriate to pray for a large share of empathy, for life in general and for our reading of the Scriptures in particular. I doubt that any calling requires a broader and deeper store of empathy, or more ability to communicate it.

Sometimes, as I stand with one foot in the religiously conservative world and the other in the liberal, I get the feeling that some preachers don't really like the Bible that much. On the one hand, there are those clergy who are more often embarrassed by the Bible than inspired by it, because they have become more critic than expositor. On the other hand, I see and hear sermons by some who speak vigorously about their love of the Bible but whose sermons show more acquaintance with books of illustrations than with the Book being expounded.

Margaret M. Mitchell noted in Harvard's 2001 Dudleian Lectures that the fourth-century preacher Chrysostom interpreted Paul not as "a depersonalized, neutral endeavor in which a person (the reader) meets an object (a written text), but rather [as] a conversation among friends." And there was a reason for this. "Chrysostom claimed that he understood Paul so well not because of his own mental acuity, or even his steadfast faith, but because he *loved* Paul so much."[5]

I won't claim that it was this that made John of Antioch "the Golden-Mouthed" (Chrysostom), but I'm sure it helped. It's hard to be eloquent about things that don't strongly grip us. With that in mind, I urge you: embrace these Bible personalities, warts and all! Lay passionate claim to Cain and Rahab, to Bartimaeus and Nicodemus. They are our spiritual kin, sometimes damned and sometimes holy, and we will understand the Scriptures and ourselves better if we claim this pantheon of belief and unbelief as our own.

Notes

1. Sean Callery, review of *The Writings of J. M. Synge* and *J. M. Synge and His World* by Robin Skelton, *The Saturday Review* 54, no. 18 (1971): 36.

2. Frederick Buechner, *Telling Secrets* (San Francisco: HarperSanFrancisco, 1991), 36-37.

3. Ibid., 84-85.

4. Gordon Reid, ed. *The Wind from the Stars: Through the Year with George MacDonald* (London: Harper Collins, 1992), 253.

5. Margaret M. Mitchell, "Pauline Palimpsests and the Protestant-Catholic Divide: The Dudleian Lecture for 2000-01," *Harvard Divinity Bulletin* (spring 2001): 11.

CHAPTER TWO

The Sacred Triangle

I dare to venture this chapter only because when I look at the nonfiction best-seller lists now and then, I am often astonished, and sometimes depressed, to see that the books on the list are so often recitations of what almost everyone already knows. This is true whether the field is business, self-help, or popular religion. We seem fascinated by the obvious, if only the outer garments are in some way new, or perhaps bizarre. So it is that I set out to tell you what, by common sense, you already know.

A good sermon involves a sacred triangle, three great love affairs. They ought to be coexisting and mutually supporting affairs, but like any love affairs they easily become competitive, and easily intrude on one another's territory. That's why I'll present them as a triangle rather than as a trinity. If we are to preach well, all of these love affairs should possess us. They should possess us as we prepare the sermon, as we preach it, and as we live afterward with its fallout.

I hate to number these love affairs, lest I seem to give them an order of preference, and thus to endorse the very danger that frightens me, namely that I make these several loves competitive. So let me say from the outset that, for matters of preaching, one is not more important than the others.

Fall in Love with the Sermon You Are Presenting

This is different from what I said in chapter 1: it isn't a matter of being in love with the Bible in general, or its characters, or its truths. As a matter of pragmatic fact, our general love is likely to be an enemy to our love for the particular sermon that we're preaching, or preparing to preach, on this particular occasion. All of us preachers know that at some point during preparation for the sermon immediately before us, we become fascinated with the possibility of a sermon we will preach later. Sometimes, in fact, we'll even be fascinated with a past sermon. This is a devilish distraction, and the preacher must resist it. Mind you, it may be rooted in truth, because the sermon before us may indeed be tedious. But the secret, of course, is to remedy these faults rather than to yearn for a better day to come or to mourn a better day past. And most of the time it isn't that this sermon is so bad; it's just that we've hit a hard place in the process of preparation.

The issue is still more crucial as we approach the pulpit. At times of a struggling psyche—an experience that comes occasionally to every preacher and that is a constant companion to some—we are tempted to look past this sermon to some future Sunday. Many a Top 25 college football team has lost its rating by looking ahead two weeks to the big game while stumbling into Backwoods State Community College. There is only one Sunday that matters—this one—and only one sermon to be preached—this one. So fall in love with this sermon.

The late Norman Vincent Peale always thought of his father, a small-town Methodist preacher, as an extraordinary man and minister. He recalls how he loved to hear his father preach: "He was thrilling because he was himself always thrilled." We're not likely to thrill others with a sermon unless we are ourselves first thrilled with it.

I admit readily that this is not easy. The preacher is obligated to feel thrilled every week, at a set time, no matter what the circumstances. This seems more than any mere mortal can manage. The great Karl Barth said that when the church bells ring on a Sunday morning, there is in the air *"expectancy* that something great, crucial and even momentous is to happen."[1] He found that momentous quality in the fact that the Bible was going to be opened, and that the preacher would then add to it something from his or her own head and heart. Well, that is an awesome prospect, but it's hard to rise to such a sense of awe through all of the average Sundays of the year—unless one is vitally restored within.

The creative experience is part of the equation. E. B. White, known to a large audience as the author of *Charlotte's Web* and other classic children's books, was one of the most significant essayists of his time. In a piece titled "How to Tell a Major Poet," White said, "All poets who, when reading from their own works, experience a choked feeling, are major." Among other things, that might remind us preachers that our sermons ought, first of all, to convict and convert us. But more than that, we ought at some point in the preparation of every sermon to feel the amazement of an idea that is bigger than we expected it to be. Some poet has referred to it as "a catch in the throat." Dale Wasserman, the man who wrote the lyrics for "The Man of La Mancha," says that at times in the writing, he could hardly believe that what he had written had come from him.[2]

But that brings us back to the dailiness (or the "weekliness") of our job. We can't announce some Sundays that we didn't get any inspiration this week—though it's possible that our congregation will sense as much before we're far into the sermon. And although many good things can be said for lectionary preaching, a serious question can be raised here. Eugene Lowry, one of the major teachers of homiletics during the past nearly thirty years, says that "in the last decade of increased mainline Protestant use of the common lectionary, sermons—on average—have become more biblical, more boring, and less evocative."[3] I think this may be partly because the text is established by the lectionary reading, and the preacher becomes the scholarly worker, doing a task with the appointed material. In fact, the sermon can easily have the feeling of a term paper come due at 11:00 A.M. Sunday. This isn't the stuff of which great worship experiences are made.

There is, you see, something to be said for the phrase one used to hear so often throughout the South: "That will preach!" The exclamation might be evoked by an anecdote, a news story, or a country-western song, but whatever, it caused creative juices to flow. I think many a lectionary preacher expects no light to come on, no compulsion to get out of the desk chair, just a labor to be performed. If that is so, the preacher must form a new spiritual and creative regimen. Whether on our knees or walking a neighborhood road, we must take hold of the text like Jacob wrestling at ford Jabbok, not knowing at first whether this stranger is God or devil, but only knowing that we must struggle until it conquers us: some word comes alive, or some phrase. Some line is reminiscent of a song we used to sing, or a conversation that long ago engaged us. Now, in the chaos, we begin to fall in love with an idea, an insight, and we can hardly wait to tell someone about it. Don't tell anyone too soon, because there's still much wrestling to be done. But you're on the right track. You have one of the love affairs of your sacred triangle.

Be in Love with the People to Whom You Preach

One of the finest moments is when a preacher can say, literally or implicitly, "I love this idea, and I love you, so I want you to have this." In truth, if something is to happen in the preaching encounter, both of these loves should be present.

The enduring entertainers have understood the importance of loving the people. Tony Bennett has spanned generations with his singing. He confesses that he still gets "butterflies" when he's going to perform; you get them, he said, "because you care. That's the most important commandment: you've got to care." Joe DiMaggio carried something of this mood to the baseball diamond. A player of effortless grace, he was once asked how he could do it day after day. DiMaggio answered, "I always thought that there was at least one person in the stands who had never seen me play, and I didn't want to let him down."

This is the mood, elevated to the issues of eternity, that has driven every good preacher—sometimes to the point that the good preacher becomes, at least for a moment, a great preacher. Charles Wesley was every inch the Oxford don, the lover of learning and sophisticated conversation; he was far removed from the poor colliers who worked England's coal mines. But he wrote, "I found the spirit of the colliers before I began to speak"; and again, "I drank into their spirit."

Clearly, this is more than sentimental feelings, more than a pleasant recollection of the nice things these people have done for us. It's the quality John Bunyan brought to his writing of *Pilgrim's Progress*. He lived with the struggles of common humanity, so he was able to speak to the souls captivated by Vanity Fair, or those mired nearly hopelessly in the Slough of Despond. As a fellow sojourner, Bunyan reached out to us and embraced us. That's the way we preachers must always feel. There must be in us something that reaches out to people—to people in general, yes, but specifically to these people sitting before us as we step into the pulpit.

This reaching out makes a communicator. It is almost impossible to preach effectively to people unless there is something in us that reaches out to them. The idealist in me wishes that this were a pure love of people, but the realist acknowledges that this love is often mixed. As a matter of painful fact, I suspect that the primary love driving some public personalities (including some preachers) is self-love: to love others for the benefit they may bring to us. This feeling is almost always a factor in any human love, since you and I are imperfect creatures, but for some it is the prevailing factor. I have no doubt but that some communicators have become very effective with no higher impulsion than this kind of self-interest. Leave them to heaven. Let us seek simply to keep our own love of people as pure as we can. Human as we are, this is an unceasing assignment.

At times, it's easier to love people in the abstract than in the particular. The philosopher can wax eloquent about the wonders of the human creature; the nurse's aide can add a quite different and compelling dimension to the philosopher's understanding. The preacher is required to combine the two viewpoints. We not only see humanity at these different levels; our theology also reminds us that we are, on the one hand, only a little lower than the angels, but also that we are decidedly fallen.

We are not naive as we look out at a congregation, but neither are we cynical. Maisie Ward, the devout Catholic laywoman who with her husband founded the Sheed and Ward publishing house, noted a generation ago that it's not true that "people are hungry for God or immortality in any conscious sense; they have starved so long they do not recognize their hunger or know what is the matter with them, or that anything is the matter."[4] It is our business to recognize, on the one hand, that most of the people to whom we preach don't show a passionate longing for God; but on the other hand, they do have a God-shaped void. And with that knowledge, we love them not only for the wondrous void (their potential), but also for the sometimes monstrous, absurd, and pathetic ways they try to fill it. One must have a great sympathy for the human race if one is to love enough to preach well to it. That sympathy may well begin with an unflinching look at ourselves.

Be in Love with Christ

Please don't think that I'm slipping into an easy piety. To love Christ is to deal with the incongruity of One who is hailed as the Lion of Judah but who appears as a slain Lamb. He is not an easy love unless we domesticate him. For though he is gentle, he is unutterably demanding: leave your home, hate your family, take up your cross. Loving him is hazardous, for knowing he is life eternal, we must give up our lives to join company with him. But love for Christ is our only safeguard against the dangers of the two loves I have already recommended. Our love for the message we deliver can easily become pride of ownership, or of our creative gifts. Our love for the people to whom we preach is always partially tainted by the pleasure we find in the adulation or loyalty we evoke. But our love for Christ, and in return, his love for us, chastens and refines our lesser loves.

As warmly as I recommend soul preaching, I know its perils. If, as Phillips Brooks said, that preaching is the communication of truth through personality, some of us ponder the profile of our personalities. When I insist that to preach well, we must deliver our own souls, I know too well that some of our souls aren't all that great. But I'm convinced that even a poor soul is better than no soul at all. And I am even more convinced that if that soul, whatever its limitations, is taken with Christ, it becomes a force with which hell must deal.

So it is that we step into a pulpit, or some reasonable facsimile thereof. We have a message; it isn't Gabriel or Chrysostom or Fosdick, but we're excited about it and thrilled to have a chance to pass it along. And we have people. A sociologist might count them quite average, but we love them. And there is Christ, a "holy passion, filling all [our] frame."[5] Something momentous is about to happen. It may never find a place even in the meanest local history, but it will have its recording in eternity.

Notes

1. Karl Barth, *The Word of God and the Word of Man,* trans. by Douglas Horton (New York: Harper, 1957), 104.

2. Minda Maver, "The Possible Dream," *On Wisconsin* 94, no. 1 (1992): 14.

3. Eugene Lowry, *The Sermon* (Nashville: Abingdon Press, 1997), 41.

4. Maisie Ward, *They Saw His Glory* (New York: Sheed and Ward, 1956), 4.

5. George Croly, "Spirit of God, Descend upon My Heart," *The United Methodist Hymnal* (Nashville: The United Methodist Publishing House, 1989), 500.

CHAPTER THREE

Where Four Ways Meet

Some years ago, I stumbled upon an old book for preachers titled *Here Is My Method: The Art of Sermon Construction*, edited by Donald Macleod. It is a collection of insights from a number of pulpiteers, and I absorbed it with fascination, just as I have speeches at any number of clergy conferences where an able preacher has shared some homiletical secrets. This is preacher talk, and we all love it. Sometimes we even learn something from it, but not often. Then why am I including such a chapter in this book? Because that's what this chapter is about, my method, even though it isn't so titled. We all like to get into such material, and if we come up with even one or two helpful insights, it's worth our time. Homiletics is a peculiar craft, and it deserves all the inquiry one can bring to it. Besides, this method has worked well for me for so long, that I can't help thinking it might help someone else.

Mind you, I didn't consciously work out this theory, nor did I find it by research. It is nothing more than the process that has developed for me over the years. Only after I began to teach preaching and was confronted by the frequent question, "How do you go about it?" did I stop to analyze what I had been doing.

This method will work for both the lectionary preacher and for those who begin with an idea. I realize that a person fully committed to lectionary preaching looks skeptically at any sermon that doesn't begin with a Scripture; I've sensed that some people who aren't sure about the inspiration of Scripture are quite committed to the inspiration of the lectionary. I'm a bit of a pragmatist about this. As I look at collections of classic sermons, I find a substantial number that quite clearly began with an idea and found their text later. The sin is not in beginning with an idea, but in misusing Scripture to fit the idea. The remedy is to know the Scriptures well enough that—even without the aid of a topical Bible—we find passages that can enter into a legitimate marriage with our insight.

The formula I offer is at its most useful in those instances when we are asked to speak for occasions other than the weekly service in the church we pastor, but it works with surprising effectiveness for the every-week preacher. It has been my experience that a sermon is best found at the intersection where four ways meet:

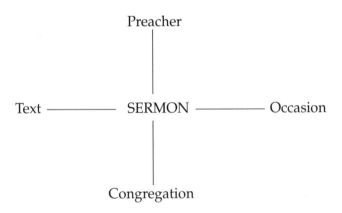

At this moment a purist might ask where the Holy Spirit fits in this diagram. In truth, where the Holy Spirit almost always comes in is somewhere in the conglomerate of our talents, our predispositions, our intelligent hearing. Only rarely, it seems to me, does the Holy Spirit move outside the rather normal channels of our personalities and the peculiar circumstances of any given time.

Preacher

The preacher would seem to need no further defining. After all, the preacher should know who he or she is. Except, of course, that we are different people on different occasions, with different congregations and with different texts. Every time I contemplate a sermon, I need to contemplate myself. I need to remember that I change as the days go by. Honestly, it seems such a short time ago that I was being introduced as "the young minister," and now people tell me how much I remind them of their grandfather. I am, indeed, a different person, and I need to be self-perceptive enough to reason how that affects the people to whom I preach and the way I approach the text.

Most of us are not too gifted at defining ourselves. Robert Burns said it so simply: "O wad some Pow'r the giftie gie us / To see oursels as others see us!"—assuring us that with such a gift we free ourselves from many a blunder. Preachers can easily overstep significant boundaries by not realizing how others see them; sometimes the "blunder" destroys the effectiveness of a given sermon, sometimes it weakens a whole ministry. A preacher is one person the first time he or she steps into a particular pulpit, and after a year of service in that church, quite a different person. This is so obvious, we're likely to miss it unless we intentionally ponder it.

Congregation

The role of the congregation, or body of people to whom we speak, is also an obvious factor, but one wouldn't guess so from seeing the way even accomplished speakers sometimes fail to adapt to audiences in different parts of the country or in different types of circumstances. The apostle Paul got the point: "I have become all things to all people, that I might by all means save some" (1 Corinthians 9:22).

The approach to the text, the title of the sermon, the illustrations used, the quotes, if any—all of these are shaped by
the nature of the audience.

And don't settle for superficial judgments. It is never
just "a youth group," it's a particular youth group. A church
in suburban Atlanta and a rural Georgia community are
both southern, but that's where the resemblance ends. As a
pastor in Cleveland I discovered that the funeral practices
in the various neighborhoods made them a thousand
miles apart, though I could travel their distance in fifteen
minutes.

So a thoughtful pastor will preach John 3:1-8 differently
if the service is in a retirement community, a new suburb
populated by young families, or a youth rally. The text is
the same, and so in a measure is the preacher, but the
makeup of the congregation shines quite different lights on
the text. A preacher may return to the text from which the
first Sunday's sermon was preached after five years in a
community, but this sermon will be very different because
the preacher_ and the congregation are quite differently
related.

Occasion

We're most conscious of the differences shaped by the
occasion when we're speaking for some community event,
celebration, or organization, but the principle operates just
as surely in one's own pulpit. The church calendar is of
course a factor, and we ought to take full advantage of it.
But the civil calendar is also an issue. The Sunday near New
Year's Day is made to order for a converting kind of preaching; whatever the text, it ought to intersect in some way
with the mood of new beginnings. All of these days carry
the quality of an occasion: Martin Luther King Day, the
Sunday nearest Independence Day, and the Sunday before
Thanksgiving.

Denominational calendars are also a factor, and local celebrations. The pastor ought always to be a cheerleader for the community the church serves; if some local event or some historical anniversary is being played up in the community, it should be in the preacher's mind during the homiletical process. And then, of course, there are local and national and international happenings that must challenge the preacher's heart and mind in the process of sermon development. I reminded a ministers' conference on an October day in 2001 that the church calendar identified the following Sunday as the eighteenth Sunday after Pentecost—but that to their people it was the fourth Sunday after the September 11th tragedy. The prophet Jeremiah saw the destruction of Jerusalem as an issue before God; any sensitive pastor will approach the pulpit at certain times with the same feeling that we must assure our people that God broods over our human distress.

Text

And then there is the text, the lesson of the day. A passage of Scripture is to be known primarily in its biblical, historical, and critical context, but the preacher who stops there abandons the prophetic calling. Our task is indeed to explain faithfully and intelligently, but our exegesis is also to an end—namely, to awaken and sustain the people of God, and to bring the reality of God to those who do not yet respond to the Eternal. Jewish tradition offers insight for this calling. It contends that every Jew was at Mount Sinai for the giving of the Torah, but the sounds resonated differently for each one. I like that. A Christian preacher will say that the Holy Spirit thus applies the text to each ready listener. I submit that we preachers ought to cooperate in this process. A text is never received nor preached in a vacuum, and the preacher who feels that his or her message is the "pure" Word of God is nothing less than presumptuous. The sermon is always colored by the conduit through which it has passed; none of us can be dispassionately objective, and when we think we are, we are most in danger of distorting the Word. So although we should avoid twisting a text to fit our purposes, we ought on the other hand to allow the text to reflect who we are, who the people are, and what the occasion is. The text can then be not only a Word from the heart of God, but also a Word with soul.

The point at which the text intersects with the other three factors makes all the difference. When I was seventeen years old, I preached for an event in Bolivar, Missouri. I preached from Genesis 32:22-32, the story of Jacob's encounter with the angel at the ford Jabbok. I've preached from the text any number of times since then; I see it as one of the seminal stories of the human showdown with God. At a time when psychological metaphors were especially popular I pictured Jacob's crisis in his acknowledgment of his name, Jacob—"heel-grabber, cheat"—and reflected on the Rumplestiltskin theory that the first step of healing is to speak the name of our sin (though the psychologist probably wouldn't use that theological term). As a guest speaker at a judicatory meeting, an Annual Conference of The United Methodist Church, I concentrated on Jacob's limp with the sermon "Coming to Conference with a Limp." When I was myself just emerging from a dark place, I pondered that the stranger wanted to leave Jacob when dawn began to break, because this is, like my sermon title, "The Night Visitor." At the height of one Olympic season, I observed that wrestling may well be the oldest of all sports, and that—by my vote, at least—Jacob was the greatest wrestler of all time. He began his wrestling career in his mother's womb, pursued it with parent, sibling, and in-laws, and never got it right until the night he lost the match at the ford Jabbok.

The text was the same. In each instance, I recited the salient details of the story (so many of the great biblical stories are unknown to most postmoderns). But each time I brought the text to a different intersection: I, the preacher, was different; so, too, was the congregation; so, too, the occasion.

The Intersection at Work

How, specifically, does the intersection work for starting the homiletical process? Let me give a lectionary example, then a nonlectionary one. The *congregation* is one for whom I have the regular oversight of souls. I, the *preacher*, am a known entity to this congregation; I have been with them long enough that they will honor my role as their teaching pastor. The *text*, from the lectionary, is Matthew 28:16-20. The *occasion* is Trinity Sunday.

With this text, one might ordinarily preach on missions, or the Great Commission. But it is Trinity Sunday, and I am in a position to teach my people regarding a major Christian doctrine. Coming to the intersection with these four particular elements, I preach on the subject, "Trinity Is an Action Word."

I'll use as a nonlectionary occasion the time I was chaplain of the week at the venerable Chautauqua Institution. I had been there before, so I knew what to expect: a magnificent Sunday morning gathering in the great amphitheater, and smaller crowds in that same setting on weekday mornings. On Sunday evening there was a vesper service in the Hall of Philosophy, a romantic setting in faux Greek architecture. Looking to the audience's left, through the open Greek sides, was a good view of Lake Chautauqua.

The *congregation* was a particularly literate group of persons, conversant with ideas, literature, culture—and religious, or perhaps sentimental, enough to invest thirty minutes in the vesper service. The *preacher* was one of the nine chaplains of the summer, chosen from many denominations in the United States and often also from Canada and the British Isles. The *occasion* was a vesper service where the ritual and all of its parts, except the Scripture and the sermon, is as it has been for over a century.

It's up to me to choose the text. Considering the setting on Lake Chautauqua, I decide to take a story from another lake, Gennesaret (Luke 5:1-11). Recalling that perhaps Garrison Keillor had performed at Chautauqua, but at least certain that nearly everyone in my audience was familiar with his keynote piece, I did a clear takeoff of his "News from Lake Woebegon": "The News from Lake Gennesaret." I followed the script, so to speak, and to my delight, they got it.

As I said before, one person's method won't necessarily work for anyone else, but the approach may quicken your thinking. In any event, it's always a wholesome exercise to ponder the occasion, to see the text in relationship to the other factors, to take a full view of the congregation, even if you've been their pastor for years, and to ask yourself who the preacher is. Some of us haven't asked ourselves that question for years, so the examination may be way overdue.

CHAPTER FOUR
If You Don't Have a Name,
How Do You Know Who You Are?

Boy and man, I've been preaching for over half of the twentieth century, and now into the twenty-first, but I'm still quite a novice at teaching preaching. I would be wise, therefore, to stay with the conventional wisdom of more experienced teachers. Nevertheless, as with all who are not as wise as the angels, I rush in with a theory of my own.

Where almost every homiletics professor says, "Get a theme sentence first," I plead, "Get a title! Don't wait too long, else it may be too late." Not so late that you can't think of one, but so late that the title will cease to fulfill its most crucial function. The purpose of a theme sentence is to focus a sermon, give it unity and coherence. The aim is right, because if there's anything a sermon ought to have, it's unity and coherence. So why do I opt rather for a title? Because I think a title does a better job of achieving these ends, and several others in the process.

Many preachers think of a title simply as something clever, to be tagged to the sermon with a close enough relationship that the preacher can't be charged with false advertising. I see the title as absolutely crucial. And while I like for it, under the best of circumstances, to be clever enough to entice listening, or to keep the kernel of the sermon alive in the listener's mind after the service is over, my purpose in the title is much more central. The title should set the boundaries for the sermon. Or to put it another way, the title should remind the preacher, all through the process of preparation, where the sermon is going, so that he or she will be able eventually to lead the congregation to the promised land of the sermon's purpose.

So why do I think a title is more effective than a theme sentence? First, because it's more succinct, more pointed. The longer a theme sentence, the more likely it is to scatter the fire. If the theme sentence becomes compound or complex, it will almost surely mean that the sermon has more than one goal in mind; or worse, that the preacher isn't really sure what the goal is. By its very succinctness, the title is more effective in maintaining the crucial element of unity. Believe me, the connecting links in most of our brains are faulty enough that they easily skip about from one idea to another. We need all the help we can get if we are to guide listeners through the labyrinth of our ideas to the destination. A good title helps immeasurably.

From a quite practical and pragmatic point of view, the title is what the congregation reads in the bulletin, sees on the screen in a "contemporary" service, or finds announced on the church bulletin board or in the newspaper church page. It's hard to imagine a theme sentence having the same exposure. More to the point, there's no need for both. If the title is what it should be, it eliminates the need for a theme sentence. It is shorthand for the theme.

Defining a Good Title

What constitutes a good title? First, and above all else, it is true to what the sermon is about. Once the preacher is satisfied about where the sermon is going, he or she must find a title that catches its essence. From that point forward, the title provides both boundaries and focus. If the title isn't true to the essence of the sermon, it's a poor title; no matter how clever, how catchy, or how memorable, it's a poor title.

Anyone who has read sermons by Harry Emerson Fosdick knows why he was the most significant pulpiteer of his generation. Even those who disagree with something of Dr. Fosdick's theology must still admire his consummate skill. Titles were a big part of this skill. He spoke often to daily human needs, and did so intelligently and with a generally solid biblical base—and almost always with a memorable title. "On Catching the Wrong Bus" took a minor newspaper story and made it a metaphor for the misuse of life. "On Making the Most of a Bad Mess" spoke to universal human experience. But his titles were just as effective when he addressed national and world affairs. At the height of Hitler's power, Dr. Fosdick chose as his title, "God Talks to a Dictator." That's a title you'll remember, and with it (assuming the sermon is reasonably good), you'll be able to capsulize the sermon. With victory at hand in World War II, Dr. Fosdick challenged his vast audience, "On Worshiping the Gods of a Beaten Enemy." I know that sermon only from reading it, but the title has become a lifelong warning for me.

Many good things could be said about these titles. But the best is simply this: they described what Dr. Fosdick was preaching about. Thus, whether you heard the sermon, or read it later, you had a better than average chance of remembering its message because the title so effectively captured the essence of the sermon.

Perhaps because of my own prejudices in the matter, I'm impressed that so many of Dr. Fosdick's titles sound like an abbreviation of his theme. Specifically, a favorite titular form for a Fosdick sermon was to begin it with the preposition "on," as in: "On Catching the Wrong Bus," or "On Making the Most of a Bad Mess." It's as if he had cast his theme as a proposition, then made that proposition into the sermon title. In any event, that succinctness put boundaries around Fosdick's insights, even as it left the listener or reader with a memorable encapsulation of what the sermon was all about in the title phrase.

Second, the title should be reasonably attractive. The Willow Creek Church, in Greater Chicago, has probably made more of a science of reaching the unchurched than any other single congregation. One of their discoveries is that of the unchurched urban dwellers, 54 percent won't come to hear a sermon until they know the title. After all, these are people who are used to choosing among movie titles, book titles, and sitcom titles. Why should we think they would turn off this habit when contemplating, even casually, the idea of church?

Our task, it seems to me, is to come up with a title that attracts but that does so with integrity. We should never be guilty of false advertising. Most of us have encountered sermons that drew us by the title, but that failed not only to fulfill the promise of the title, but also failed even to expound on the subject the title suggested. And may the Lord save us from titles that play on sensation. We associate this matter with a certain type of evangelist or television preacher, but any creative preacher is susceptible to the temptation. Of course, taste is often the perception of the individual. What seems inappropriate and unduly sensational to me may seem quite engaging to someone else.

Some titles attract because they promise something in which we're already interested. This is especially true of the various "How to" titles: "Seven Secrets of a Happy Home"; "How to Be a Winner"; "The Way to Victorious Living." A pulpit giant of two generations ago, Arthur John Gossip, used such a "helpful" theme with his sermon, "How Others Gained Their Courage." On the other hand, some titles get their power by being enigmatic.

Perhaps one will remember the phrase ever after because of the way the sermon printed it on the mind, but before hearing the sermon, the title meant nothing; it drew us, perhaps by its euphony, or by some indelible intrigue. One thinks of a movie title like *The Shawshank Redemption*: the peculiar phrase pulled us, we knew not why, but now the title is inseparable from the movie. When people tell me, forty years later, that they still remember, "Irony in the Corner Drug Store," I know a phrase that revealed nothing before the sermon, made an indelible impact.

We should usually avoid titles that are so broad and all-embracing that they become generic. "The Importance of Faith" means nothing; and worse, it empowers the preacher to roam the whole of Montana. "How to Be Saved" will draw only two kinds of persons: the faithful who will come to their church no matter what, and an exceedingly rare person who wants to be saved and who knows it. Yes, I know that Billy Graham's sermon titles are usually in this quite generic style; but he's Billy Graham, and people are attending or tuning in because they see him as an authority on whatever subject is announced. Probably the very factor that makes such a title fail for most of us makes it succeed for him. The editor of a homiletical publication urges his potential writers to seek "attention-getting titles. Not 'The Goodness of God,' but 'The Goodness That Roared.'"[1]

Now and then the culture around us provides a title, by way of a popular phrase, a book, a song. This was more often the case a short generation ago, when our common culture was more truly common; today we're so bifurcated that it's not easy to find a phrase that "belongs" to everyone. At another time I preached on a song title, "I've Got to Be Me," and knew that almost all of my hearers above the age of ten would plug in with me. It would be difficult to find such a popular song today that would cut across age, ethnic, and artistic lines. But we still have such phrases at one point or another in our culture. So the remarkable Episcopal woman cleric Fleming Rutledge captures our interest with the simple phrase, "Flying First Class." In the process, such a title helps make the sermon itself easier to remember.

A third quality of a good title, that it is reasonably memorable. Because if the title is memorable, there's an equally good chance that the sermon itself will stay with the hearer. Here again I think of a Fosdick title, "The Importance of Doubting Our Doubts"; such a phrase makes it very likely that a thoughtful listener will be able, even years later, to reconstruct the essence of what was said. I think that wouldn't be true if the title were, "The Dangers of Doubting." Sometimes the memorable quality will come by turning a subject on its head. So Fleming Rutledge chose, "No Religion Here Today." Even a religious cynic would be tempted by that or Dr. Fosdick's "The Danger of Going to Church"! Fosdick's "The Great Christ and the Little Churches" told where he was going, yet still compelled one to want to hear.

In his fine book, *Preaching Without Notes*, Joseph M. Webb emphasizes the importance of sermon titles. He observes, "Too often, sermon titles are throwaways—too hackneyed, too clichéd, too theological, too ambiguous, too cute, too nonsensical."[2] I concur! But I must also confess that good titles are not easy to come by. Somerset Maugham was the kind of person around whom apocryphal tales grew easily and abundantly, so I can't promise that this is a true story, but it's quite believable. A young writer approached Maugham for help in getting a title for his story. Maugham asked, "Does your story have any drums?" "No." "Any bugles?" Again, the answer was no. "Well, then, it's easy," Maugham said. "Call your story 'No Drums, No Bugles.' "[3] I'm sure I've encountered sermon titles developed by just such specious logic. No matter! Even the most egregious creative failures don't change the basic fact: a good title is the preacher's most effective instrument for giving a sermon focus and boundaries; and if the preacher is fortunate, the title may also have qualities that will make the sermon more attractive and memorable. Not many uses of half-a-dozen or so words can make such dramatic claims.

Notes

1. Stanley Purdum, ed. *Proclaim,* in an instruction sheet for writers.

2. Joseph M. Webb, *Preaching Without Notes* (Nashville: Abingdon Press, 2001), 74.

3. Frank C. Wilson, *Symbols and Symptoms* (Indianapolis: Guild Press of Indiana, 1995), 37.

CHAPTER FIVE

Knowing Where You're Going—
And Taking Someone with You

Nearly every day someone tells us, directly or indirectly, that the Western world is now a mission field; we can't assume, as our pulpit ancestors did, that people know the Bible, are predisposed toward the church, or have any understanding of what Christianity means. No element in the sermon demonstrates this change as clearly as the introduction.

When I read the great sermons of a century ago, or even of fifty years ago, I am astonished by the way the preacher simply jumped into the biblical text. The preacher assumed not only that people had some background knowledge of the Bible, but also that they were interested, and that the sermon could therefore build on that assumption. In 1928, Harry Emerson Fosdick threw down a gauntlet to his pulpit colleagues in his article, "What Is the Matter with Preaching?" Published in *Harper's*, one of the major thoughtful magazines of that day (and of our own), perhaps its most impelling sentence was this: "Only the preacher proceeds still upon the idea that folk come to church desperately anxious to discover what happened to the Jebusites." Fosdick went farther than that: "Who seriously supposes that . . . one in a hundred of the congregation cares . . . what Moses, Isaiah, Paul, or John meant in those special verses?"[1]

And yet, now and again Dr. Fosdick began his sermons with an immediate reference to the Bible. "Our subject suggests at once a verse in the Epistle to the Colossians"; and again, "Luke's Gospel tells us that . . . " Very few preachers would dare to begin that way today. Mind you, some don't realize the problem, so they're doing what they've always done, not thinking about whether they have the attention of any large number of those to whom they're speaking. The major difference is this, that in another day it was enough if the sermon's introduction introduced the sermon; now the introduction bears an earlier, more complicated responsibility; it must persuade those present that they are interested in the subject, and that it is to their advantage that they listen.

Let me interrupt myself momentarily to emphasize that my subject just now is the introduction to the sermon, not the kind of casual, friendly, incidental remarks that are often engaged in before the speaker gets into the real business of the day. Mind you, these remarks often have their place, especially for a guest speaker. Indeed, they are almost essential for the pulpit guest. They are meant to establish a relationship between the assembled body and the speaker, and as such they are as much a matter of courtesy as of good sense. These remarks should be comfortable, they should be complementary (to the community, the congregation, the host pastor, the musicians—though not everyone, and not overmuch!), and they should, if possible, be gently humorous. People hear a speaker better after they know him or her, and they know us better after they have laughed with us—or, perhaps, at us. Self-deprecating humor is especially appealing in this regard. But such introductory remarks are not to be confused with the introduction to the sermon.

The business of the introduction is not simply to lead persons into the sermon, but to make them want to be led. We can't assume that the people who look up at us are all that excited about hearing from us. We often discover, to our disappointment, that even the most faithful attendees don't necessarily take the sermonic enterprise that seriously. One Sunday when I was headed toward the door of a church I often attend, I found myself walking through the parking lot with an elderly man. As we chatted, he mentioned that he was hard of hearing, to the point of missing much of the sermon. I commiserated with his problem, but he quickly relieved my concern. "I don't mind," he said. "I've gone to church all of my life, and I've found that they generally say about the same thing every Sunday." His comment was a painful indictment of standard pulpit fare, but also a reminder that the presence of warm bodies is no promise of engaged minds. When we look out upon a pleasant gathering, we need to remind ourselves that the good attendance means we've won not quite half the battle. The most crucial encounters are still ahead.

I have come to look upon the sermon introduction as remarkably akin to the social introduction. When I find myself introducing two of my friends to each other, my challenge is to find an area that gives them reason to see the introduction as more than just a polite handshake. "Bill and Harry, I've been wanting to introduce the two of you to each other because I know that you're both great professional football fans. And if I'm correct, you're both disillusioned Steelers fans. You have a lot in common."

With the sermon introduction I'm saying, though not in so many words, "Sermon and People, I really want you to know one another." It's quite possible that my people aren't favorably disposed to my sermon, especially if the sermon has to do with something of such marginal interest as tithing, community responsibility, or sacrificial living. The introduction may therefore call for some extraordinary gifts of subtlety and endearment. But that's the point—we can't always preach what people want to hear; indeed, we shouldn't even try, lest we lose our prophetic credentials. But we do want the sermon to be heard, and that won't happen (especially with unattractive themes) unless we entice interest at the outset. So my business, in the introduction, is first of all, to introduce two dear friends—the congregation I love, and the sermon I love.

In other generations, including the one in which I learned public address and preaching, we were often encouraged to make the first sentence compelling and memorable. This idea isn't to be altogether discounted, but I doubt that it is as universally effective as it was in other days. I think first sentences are lost on many persons nowadays. As I travel from one pulpit to another, I find that a good many congregations need a moment or two to settle in—time to adjust clothing, take a handkerchief from a purse, say a word to a family member or a friend. Mind you, I find that some churches are so accustomed to pulpit expectancy that they are ready when I am. That's a happy state, and a faithful, able pastor can eventually help a congregation to such a habit, but it may take time. Meanwhile, a more gentle entry may be more effective. I'm not recommending a throwaway sentence at the beginning, but neither would I, in most cases, invest my whole soul in this sentence.

Qualities of a Good Sermon Introduction

First and foremost, a good introduction should be intimately related to the subject of the sermon. This is so obvious, so commonsense, that I would be embarrassed to say it if it weren't that so few introductions accomplish it. Quite simply, an introduction is no good unless it introduces. It ought to engage the audience, yes; but to a purpose, to their getting involved in the sermon proper. A fascinating story, an intriguing quote, and a clever joke don't accomplish anything unless they lead us into the sermon. "Ah, but I got their interest," the preacher says of some idle story. But to what end? I have heard too many sermons where listeners remembered nothing but the opening joke. And I've heard almost as many sermons where the preacher made an earnest but somewhat absurd attempt to connect the joke with the sermon when it is altogether obvious that there is no relationship. Such introductions are worse than nothing; they not only do not introduce the subject, but also they lead people up another path so they may never join us in the pursuit of the day.

I'm not suggesting that the introduction should always have a transparent connection to what follows. To the contrary, some of the best introductions may seem quite unrelated, so that a prosaic listener may look again at the title listed in the bulletin, wondering whether the preacher has changed topics. But the preacher had better know that the connection is there, and that in time everyone will know that it is.

A second rule is also obvious, and nevertheless, often ignored. The introduction ought to consist of a single thought. The introduction is not the place for complexity. Some subjects demand complexity in the body of the material, but listeners aren't ready for complexity as the sermon begins; indeed, complexity is likely to discourage them from listening.

Peter Marshall, late chaplain of the United States Senate and minister at New York Avenue Presbyterian Church in Washington, D.C., was especially skilled at moving gracefully, yet directly and unerringly, to the body of his sermon. I find in reading numbers of his sermons that he had, within a minute-and-a-half or two minutes, gone from his opening sentence into the heart of his sermon's purpose.[2] Yet there is no sense of haste. When the driver knows where he or she is going, the passengers can ride leisurely.

A third rule follows hard on the second; the introduction should usually be brief. In my judgment, however, we should have a good bit of variance here, because the length of the introduction is influenced so much by the sermon's subject matter. An old rule of thumb suggested that the introduction take up roughly one-seventh of the sermon, but I wouldn't fight for that figure. And sometimes, in sermons built on the narrative model, the introduction flows so smoothly into the body that even the writer finds it hard to say where one ends and the other begins. On the other hand, a sermon that requires a good deal of explanatory background material may unfold very slowly.

The greatest danger of length that I observe sometimes in myself and sometimes in my students is the temptation to linger unnecessarily on material where the speaker feels very much at home. Two or three "for instances" are more than enough to lead the listeners into more substantive matters, but because the speaker finds five or six such examples, he or she is somehow compelled to list them all. In the process an audience is in danger either of tedium, or of distraction. The basic rule, once again, is that the introduction serves its purpose only as it introduces. If it becomes an end in itself, it fails as an introduction. Obviously, the whole sermon should be carefully prepared, but if there is a single portion that deserves that attention more than any other, it is the introduction.

The fourth major rule is prepare the introduction with special care. No wasted words here, no fumbling about. The speaker may seem to be very casual, very low key, but never out of control. On the whole, I don't favor memorizing a sermon, even though I plead strongly for preaching without notes or manuscript. However, if any part of a sermon is justifiably memorized, it is the few opening sentences. In any event, a preacher must not seem dependent on notes or manuscript in the opening several minutes. This is no time for looking down; it is the time for direct, eye-to-eye communication, for a feeling of immediacy and intimacy, because it is here that the preacher and the people begin to establish their relationship. If the preacher is tentative, or more taken with manuscript and notes than with the people, the relationship is put at a disadvantage. So let the introduction be particularly well-crafted, and let the preacher deliver it cleanly. Sometimes the preacher reasons that because the sermon begins with a story, it need not be written out. To the contrary! A story that is told with dozens of unnecessary words and circumlocutions quickly becomes as dull as a friend's recounting of a "I said, then she said" conversation. Make every word count in the introduction, without sounding stilted or rehearsed.

And of course, rule five: the introduction should arouse curiosity and interest. Most worshipers come to the sermon willing to listen, but also with several competing thoughts on their minds. The preacher's task is to make the sermon more interesting than those other matters, and that can be quite an assignment. There are many ways to do this. Sometimes a statistic, perhaps especially one with a touch of humor, yet with a potential point: "Did you know there are more plastic flamingos in the United States than real ones?" Or perhaps, "Here's something to ponder: an average person has 696 muscles, while a caterpillar has more than 4,000." Be sure your statistic is going somewhere! Be sure that it is truly related to the sermon that follows.

A striking quote can also be effective. Try Orson Welles, legendary film director: "I hate television. . . . I hate it as much as peanuts. But I can't stop eating peanuts." Or perhaps a quote that you intend to argue with as the sermon unfolds: "A thoughtful man said of his denomination, the Church of England, that it was like 'an elderly lady, who mutters away to herself in a corner, ignored most of the time.' The person who said it? George Carey, who was then head of that body, as the Archbishop of Canterbury." Or perhaps a mild shocker: "We preachers don't often quote striptease artists, at least not from the pulpit. But Gypsy Rose Lee, perhaps the most famous of her kind, is supposed to have said, 'God is love, but get it in writing.' " Those of us who love words (and that ought to include all preachers) must be careful not to begin with a quote that is so subtle that people don't get it. Obviously, such a quote fails the very purpose of an introduction.

Many preachers, when they think of matters to arouse curiosity and evoke interest, think immediately of a story, or of an apt illustration. Their instincts are right, but the application is often regretful. There's a tendency to over-long stories, so that the story becomes a destination rather than a path into the sermon. Many a preacher works so hard at getting a good opening story, that the story is the only memorable thing about the sermon. An opening story should be succinct, have human appeal, and move faith-fully toward the body of the sermon proper.

There is a type of preacher who likes to begin a sermon with a question that calls for a physical response from the audience. "How many of you here have ever felt frightened on a dark night? Raise your hands." I react badly to that sort of approach, because I feel the speaker is intruding on my privacy. I'm not ready for such an invasion at the very beginning of the sermon-relationship; let the speaker earn the right to consider me such a confidant. Better to say, "I've often been frightened on a dark night. Perhaps, under the worst of circumstances, you have, too." Better for the speaker to be vulnerable than to ask the congregation to be vulnerable—especially at the early-friendship stage of the introduction.

If there is any single approach that is particularly reliable, it is the personal story or the personal reference. I say this with great uneasiness, knowing that the very term will turn off some of my colleagues, and knowing on the other hand that it will encourage others in bad practices. Let me begin to make my point with counsel from Sloan Wilson, a popu-lar novelist who was substantial enough to give a charac-terization and a phrase to a period of the twentieth century with the title of one of his novels, *The Man in the Gray*

Flannel Suit. Wilson said, "Anyone who tries to tell the truth about himself is interesting." Then he warned that the bore who talks about himself, is boring because he makes himself "the hero of every encounter."[3]

So I am emphatically not wanting to encourage those persons who simply delight in talking about themselves, and who engage in shameless name-dropping, self-aggrandizement, or wearisome reminiscing about themselves, their spouse, or their children. Such pulpit fare is not only tedious, it may become downright wicked.

However, these various misuses don't discredit a good practice. In simple fact, the person standing in the pulpit is interesting to the people in the pew. This is a live person; perhaps not an authority on anything, but present and real, which cannot be said for the person the preacher might otherwise quote. I might begin a sermon by saying, "Ralph Waldo Emerson said 'There is properly no history; only biography.' " But I make the introduction more compelling if I begin, "I love history. That probably already makes me seem odd to some of you, but I confess it readily. I want to add, however, in the next breath, that I think history comes into its own in a special way through the biographies of those persons who make the history. I think that's something like what Emerson had in mind when he said 'There is properly no history; only biography.' " Now obviously I'm not in any way to be classified with Emerson, but that's partly why the listeners are more interested in me—and even more so when I speak in a self-deprecating way.

Statements such as "I didn't know much at fifteen, but I thought I knew this much . . . ." leave listeners wanting to hear more. Or, "I grew up in the Great Depression (or, the baby boomer generation, or generation X)": immediately some in the congregation count you as their own, and others wait to hear what characterizes your generation from your point of view. But never tell someone else's story as if it happened to you. There must be a place in Dante's

Inferno for those who do such a thing; if not, I'm going to petition that a special section be added.

Faults to Avoid

Some matters of both content and style ought to be avoided in the introduction: for one, an argumentative manner or contentious statement. There are probably instances where a speaker may gain attention by establishing an adversarial position, but they are few. Generally speaking, it's better to have people on your side at the outset, and generally speaking, they aren't ready to deal with an argumentative pulpit before they've fully settled into the listening mode.

For the same reason, avoid broad gestures in the first minutes. Such physical patterns may have a place a little farther into the sermon, but the audience isn't ready for such enthusiasm so early. We've been living with the sermon for days, perhaps weeks or months, so we've built up an excitement (surely, please!); furthermore, we know the end from the beginning. But our listeners know none of this, so they're not ready for expansive gestures, nor for a loud voice. I remember the counsel we street corner preachers used to receive a very long generation ago: "Start low, begin slow, rise higher, take fire." This is still good advice for the preacher's manner in the introduction.

And as I indicated earlier, beware of the "funny story" that isn't honestly related to the sermon. It is dangerous at both ends of the spectrum. If it's a poor joke, we're off to a bumbling start; if it's a successful joke, the people may never get past it to the weightier matters of the sermon. Avoid beginning with an apology. There are exceptions to this rule, as to almost every rule. But on the whole, apologies—especially at the outset of the sermon—are bad business. They may evoke sympathy, or worse, pity, but these are not good foundations for effective listening. This warning includes those veiled apologies, such as the "I've had such a busy week" stuff. A good share of the people listening feel that they, too, have had a busy week, but they've still been expected to deliver their quota. Now it's the preacher's turn.

As You Approach the Pulpit

The sermon begins long before we say some liturgical words that officially declare it to be so. If there is a processional, the people have seen us singing or not singing, glad or depressed; in a more informal setting, the preacher may circulate before the service, greeting people; in such, the sermon has begun, realized or not.

But something particularly significant is at stake as the preacher steps into the pulpit. This is a time for strength and assurance. People look for strength—not arrogance, which is a sign of weakness or imperception, but *strength*. They want to feel that the person who is about to deliver the Word of the Lord is sure of his or her identity. The preacher should be confident and self-assured; or more significantly, if you prefer, God-assured. He or she should be comfortable in the assignment; if the preacher is ill at ease, the feeling will spread to the congregation. Remind yourself that the people want you to succeed. It's painful to sit in the pew and watch someone die in the pulpit; sometimes more painful for the people in the pew, believe it or not, than for the one dying. I'm sure there are churches where a segment of the membership is so desirous of a change in leadership that some may enjoy seeing the preacher thrown for a loss, but these folks are very few. People gain strength from our strength, confidence from our confidence.

Remember that you are in charge as you begin to preach. If there's any doubt in your mind, recite the evidence. First, you are called. Even if you don't feel it at this moment, you once felt it, and felt it enough to turn your whole life in this direction. Second, you're the scheduled preacher for this occasion. It says so somewhere: on the church bulletin board, in the order of worship, or by common consent. Third, you have something to say (this may be the weakest of the supports, and if so, you'll have to do something about it). And fourth, God wants you here, at this moment, with these people. Now, *preach.*

Let the Dog Swallow Its Tail

Half a century ago, I read a piece in a writer's magazine about article writing. I regret that I didn't save the article, nor do I remember the author; I wish I could give proper credit. But the idea has stuck with me and has informed my preaching over the years. Find a good title for your article, the writer advised, then bring the title into some early paragraph, either specifically or by clear inference; unfold your idea through the body of the piece, then come back to the title in the conclusion. Thus, "the dog swallows its tail."

This structure can be especially effective if the introduction is a story that you leave unfinished, and to which you return in the conclusion. But in every event, this structure helps enforce unity—a quality that, I repeat, is essential, yet difficult to maintain—and it adds coherence. With all of that, there is a better-than-average chance that the listener will remember your core idea, since you have packaged it so well. And that, of course, is what the introduction is about: getting people interested in the heart of the sermon, and engaging them in such a way that they make the whole sermonic trip with you.

Notes

1. Henry Emerson Fosdick, "What Is the Matter with Preaching?" *Harper's Magazine* 157 (July 1928): 135, quoted in Lionel Crocker, ed. *Harry Emerson Fosdick's Art of Preaching* (Springfield, Ill.: Charles C. Thomas, 1971), 30.

2. Peter Marshall, *Mr. Jones, Meet the Master: Sermons and Prayers of Peter Marshall* (Boston: G. K. Hall, 1973).

3. Sloan Wilson, "Explore Your Own World," *The Writer* 91 no. 7 (1978): 12.

CHAPTER SIX

The Preacher as Debater, Storyteller, and Teacher

The purpose of the introduction is to engage listeners in the topic of the day. Let us assume that we have been successful in this opening effort, that the people are with us as we move into what rhetoricians call the sermon's body. What shall we do, now that we're here? This portion of the sermon is usually the part in which we've invested the most time and research. We have some exegetical material, some illustrations, some quotes, some stimulating insights. Now, how to package them in such a way that we don't lose the interest we have developed, and that we accomplish the ends we had in mind when this message first captured our hearts and minds?

Qualities of a Good Sermon Body

Before I go into the possible methods of development, let me dare again to do a quite basic thing and list some qualities that ought to be in the body.

The first, almost surely, is *order*. Order is a noble beast of burden. We rarely seek it the way we seek other factors; yet unless the sermon has order, the other elements may well be wasted. When Edmund Burke said, "Good order is the foundation of all good things," he was speaking particularly of political order, but I'm quite sure he meant "all" when he said it, careful writer that he was. Order implies logic; if logic is missing in the order, then it is disorderly. But for the speaker, the logic is often emotional as much as it is intellectual. Sometimes we unfold our points not in the cold order a logician would recommend, but in the style of a poet or a romantic. Be sure that order exists; and although, with time, most of us find the order of our structures almost intuitively, never stop examining your decisions.

Second, *unity* will come out of the structure if the structure is truly orderly. Again, this is not a glamorous quality, and in seeking unity the preacher feels more like an engineer than a poet. Fair enough; but remember that any poem worth remembering usually has a unifying center. Conventional homiletics finds this unity in the theme sentence; I find it in the title.

Clarity is a third essential. Sometimes it's hard to come by because we aren't ourselves sure of what we're trying to say. "And if the bugle gives an indistinct sound," the apostle warned, "who will get ready for battle?" (1 Corinthians 14:8). Clarity is first of all knowing what we want to say, but it is also finding the choice words to say it. Vague and obscure words can make a clear idea difficult to understand. We preachers have a disadvantage at this point. We're part of what is called "a learned profession." Thus we can easily lose ourselves in our professional vocabulary; incidentally, this is true clear across the theological spectrum.

The body, if it is good, will also be marked, fourth, by *selection*. If one reads a text carefully, more ideas come to mind than can rightly be used in a given sermon. And some of them are very good ideas; it's just that they're not good for this sermon. Save them; you'll be preaching again next week. So, too, with illustrative matter: preachers are easily afflicted with the "kitchen sink" attitude, reasoning that if two illustrations are good, three would be even better. Someone has said that the first rule of art is exclusion: knowing what to leave out. Add a few baubles to Mona Lisa, put a vase and flowers beside her, and you have a picture that was lost in a secondhand shop centuries ago. The artist has to know what to leave out. One should use only what furthers the subject, and no more.

Fifth, the body of the sermon should be *interesting.* Most of us have heard sermons by preachers who apparently didn't realize the importance of being interesting. Again, we preachers have a particular problem; because we are specialists, we find high interest in matters that appeal very little to a person outside our specialty. Dick Feagler may well be the longest-running newspaper columnist in any major American city. He has served with several papers, but always in the Greater Cleveland, Ohio, area. His genius? "I try to write something so the guy out in Parma [a working class Cleveland suburb] will say to his wife, 'Hey, this is just what we were talkin' about last night!' It doesn't get more noble than that."[1] The way to stay interesting is to stay close to people. It is hundreds of times better than scanning the Internet for "new" illustrations.

Sixth, the material in the body should be *persuasive.* Classic books on public address often referred to the body of the speech as "the proof." Even when we feel that our aim is to inform rather than to convince or persuade, a persuasive quality is essential. I think I am not overstating the matter when I say that the difference between a sermon and a lecture is this distinction: a lecture is content to convey information, while a sermon seems, by its history and nature, to call for some sort of decision or action. So even the sermon that seems primarily to inform, informs to an end. We expect that the data we have delivered to our hearers will bring some change to them, whether in action, conduct, or attitude. After all, if someone moves from fear to confidence, or from despair to hope, something quite persuasive has happened—indeed, something converting.

Seventh, the body should especially have a quality of *freshness.* If people have the feeling they'll be hearing the "same old thing" each Sunday, they will tune us out even as they look dutifully at our faces. And they're right in doing so. One has only so much time to spend on this earth, so it's a poor stewardship of time to waste it in hearing (as one perceives it) what one already knows. It's true, of course, that the basics of our faith and of its claims are really relatively few, so of course we're compelled to repeat familiar themes. But we must declare them in a fashion that intrigues by its freshness. This sense of freshness is as essential to the preacher as to the hearer; indeed, more so. A new idea has wonderfully invigorating powers. I am repeatedly astonished by the way sermon preparation comes alive when some aspect of a text strikes me with new force. Moments before, preparation was hard slogging; now the feet of the gospel take wing.

Mind you, I'm not calling for the bizarre. Nor should we strain the basic purpose and direction of the text. But when the first-century hearers said of our Lord, "Never has anyone spoken like this" (John 7:46), I think it was not only Jesus' charisma or the presence of the Holy Spirit. Somehow he brought some unfamiliar shadings and lightings to the familiar Scriptures.

Structures of the Sermon Body

Different homileticians and preachers have come up with varieties of forms for the body of the sermon. I hate to muddy the waters still further, even in my attempt to simplify, but of course I shall now do so. I submit that there are only three basic ways to develop a sermon. One can give them different names, and come up with several more possibilities, but I'm satisfied that the "other" possibilities are nothing more than subdivisions of the big three: the linear sermon, the narrative sermon, and the line-by-line exposition.

Before going farther, let me contend that, whatever the structure, there should always be some sense of the unfolding of the idea. Peter De Vries, the twentieth-century novelist who sometimes charmed more by his puns and his wordplay than by his plots, once said "Every novel should have a beginning, a muddle, and an end." The principle works well for a sermon. In fact, as De Vries was raised in a devout Calvinist home, it may be that he got his idea from some of the sermons he heard.

A good sermon ought to have the feeling of progress. This feeling is easier to bring about in a narrative structure, but it is just as essential in a linear sermon or a line-by-line exposition. It is the feeling that the sermon is going somewhere. It is not simply a collection of facts and illustrations, but facts and illustrations that proceed with some kind of logical progression. Eugene Lowry has said in lectures that in many a three-point sermon, the points could be thrown in the air, then picked up randomly, because there is no movement from one point to another. The order could as well be 3-1-2 as 1-2-3. Needless to say, he disapproves of such. In the sermon, whatever its structure, the middle should be a muddle, and logic should lead to the promised land of the conclusion.

The Linear Sermon: The Preacher as Debater

Although students of preaching say that narrative preaching is the great, new thing, I find that among evangelical preachers and homiletical publications aimed at evangelical subscribers, the linear style is still alive and, occasionally, well. Indeed, it has found new life, of a sort, in many of the megachurches that provide their listeners with an outline of blank lines, where listeners can fill in the points of the sermon. Sometimes, for assurance, the listeners are assisted by having the first letter for the blank.

The linear structure is characterized by its use of visible points. They can number from one to seven or eight, but the preferred number is three. If done well, the points are emphasized; sometimes the preacher employs alliteration, so that each point begins with the same letter or even the same word. Every sermon ought to have an outline, but the outline is more important in a linear sermon. This is the kind of sermon that evoked the homiletical theory, "First, I tells them what I'm going to do, then I tells them, then I tells them what I told them." The linear structure reveals the points, in some measure, in the introduction, develops the points in the body (often repeating the point as one unit ends and another begins), and frequently summarizes the points as part of the conclusion.

The linear style appeals to some for its tidiness, and the sense of order that it provides. Mind you, the order is sometimes more sense than substance, but preachers and hearers alike are comforted by this sense. This structure works equally well for a topical sermon or a biblical one. Sometimes, in my prejudiced observing, the linear sermon is almost purely topical, but with a judicious sprinkling of Scripture references, to give the impression of biblical intent—this is the style of the debater. I learned it well in my high school and university days with debate teams. This style makes points in a case to be proved. It is reasoned discourse. Rhetoricians tell us that it came to us from the Greeks. There's no doubt but that it's not the style of the Hebrews, especially not as we know their style in the Old Testament. Very rarely does the Bible give us a natural outline; the preacher finds an outline that was probably not in the mind of the author. Often, we observe that the preacher simply imposes an outline upon a passage, sometimes well and sometimes not well.

Some subjects respond especially well to the linear approach. "How to" sermons surely do; indeed, their very titles often presuppose a linear style, with "Three Rules for a Happy Home" or "The Five Secrets of Victorious Living." In such instances we know not only that the style will be linear, we even know in advance the number of points. Doctrinal and apologetic sermons also fit well into the linear style, as do didactic or teaching sermons. I think it is this type of didactic sermon that has become popular in many megachurch settings.

Many very great preachers have employed the linear style, some of them exclusively. Indeed, there are preachers who don't believe a sermon is truly a sermon unless it employs several highly visible points. But there are problems: it's more difficult to maintain unity in a linear sermon. After all, if there are several declared points it is very easy for a listener, drifting in and out of consciousness, to perceive one of these points as the point of the whole sermon. And frankly, it's sometimes like that because the preacher, in the preparation process, has found it difficult to keep the various points aimed toward the major point.

Suspense is almost impossible to maintain in a linear sermon. How can there be suspense when you've already told the audience what the sermon is going to be about? As a result, the linear style is more effective with a friendly audience, where the people want to hear the preacher's thoughts on a given subject, and where they're willing to keep listening after they know what the sermon is about. This style works well when a congregation feels great loyalty to its pastor; it is less effective with those who are simply church shopping or who have no particular reason to listen to a given preacher.

If a person chooses to use the linear style, several suggestions are in order. The points should be kept as simple and succinct as possible. Since your points are meant to be visible, emphasize them; keep them clear and in the mind of the hearers. Be sure the outline comes out of the text, rather than being imposed upon it, and be sure the material under each point is linked in a significant way to that point. If you find that an illustration can easily be transferred from one point to another, your outline is suspect; either the points are too similar, or the illustrations are not definitive.

The points are stronger if they have symmetry. That is, if point one is "Watch out for despair," you don't want to phrase point two as "Shame defeats many people." I regret to report that I've heard and seen just such asymmetrical structures. In the same fashion, it's good for the points to have balance—not only in their form, but also in the length of time and amount of material given to their development. The exception to this is that the last point may profitably be shorter. Alliteration is sometimes helpful, but it is easily overdone, it is sometimes a bit too cute, and the mnemonic value is generally overrated. Be careful lest you sacrifice the true content of your passage to your desire to alliterate.

Because of my commitment to biblical preaching, and my desire for us to develop biblically literate congregations, I'm not enthusiastic about topical sermons. But there is a place for topical sermons from time to time—that is, sermons that find their source in a topic rather than in a pericope—and when a sermon is topical, the linear structure is particularly effective.

The Narrative Sermon: The Preacher as Storyteller

The narrative sermon is one in which the preacher unfolds a story. It is almost surely a one-point sermon. It's logical, but logical in the ways a plot is logical, not the way a legal brief is logical. It has an outline, but its outline is closer to the works of O. Henry or to John Updike than to the president's State of the Union address. The outline in a linear sermon is like the frame of a building when it's going up, while the outline in a narrative sermon is like bones in a body. The simple lines of a building frame are beautiful, but if the bones stick out of a body, the body ceases to be beautiful. A sermon is not narrative in style just because the preacher tells a number of stories. On the contrary, a true narrative sermon may well have only one story, namely, the story implicit in the text. Narrative sermons can be more biblical than many linear sermons, because they rely on the story in the text rather than on illustrations about the text. As Eugene H. Peterson, who has given us a vigorous vernacular Bible in *The Message,* puts it, the gospel "comes through the story of Jesus, not through the doctrine of Jesus. He was born, he lives, he dies, he rises again—it's all story. It's very important to keep the story and not just distill ideas out of it."[2]

The premier biblical example of a narrative sermon is the prophet Nathan's message to King David after David's sins concerning Bathsheba and Uriah. Nathan tells a story— apparently a very innocent one—about a rich landholder who takes unconscionable advantage of his poor neighbor. When David is angered by the story, and pronounces judgment on the villain, Nathan replies, "You are the man!" (2 Samuel 12:1-15).

Jesus uses the same device in several parables. When the Pharisees and scribes "were grumbling" about his association with sinners, Jesus "told them this parable" (Luke 15:2-3). Luke proceeds to give us three parables about God's feelings toward the lost. What Luke doesn't tell us is how Jesus' enemies responded to the series, particularly the concluding portion about the older brother (Luke 15:11-32). This concluding portion is not only a graphic portrayal of the critics, but also it is the whole point of the three stories. In the parable of the wicked tenants, Jesus is still more direct, and this time, Matthew reports, the Pharisees and chief priests "realized that he was speaking about them."

Unlike repentant David, this group "wanted to arrest him" (Matthew 21:45-46).

In my judgment, there is a narrative plot in every pericope. Some are obvious, of course, as in the instances of stories. But a plot is implicit in every kind of passage (law, wisdom, prophet, epistle), because no passage exists in a vacuum. There's a story behind each declarative statement, whether it is the commandment, "Thou shalt have no other gods before me," or Paul's appeal, "I wish you would bear with me in a little foolishness" (2 Corinthians 11:1).

Let me insist on some things that, as I see it, are *not* biblical narrative. Simply retelling a biblical story, for example, is not a narrative sermon. Nor does the retelling become a narrative sermon by the preacher's putting it in modern language, so that the far country of the prodigal son is Las Vegas, his suits Hart Shaffner & Marx, and his pigpen job a modern garbage truck. Nor is it a linear sermon with an especially large collection of illustrations. A sermon which qualifies as biblical narrative finds its structure in a plot, and the plot leads to a compelling point. In the case of Nathan's sermon, David gets the point but doesn't realize that he *is* the point until Nathan says so. Jesus never explained the point in his parables; he trusted the intelligence of his hearers more than most contemporary preachers do. Hearers either got it, or they didn't.

Narrative Forms

A narrative sermon can take a surprising variety of forms. The easiest, of course, is a single biblical story—Daniel in the lion's den, for instance. But you must find the plot in the story, and by the plot I'm not referring simply to the Bible story itself, but to the way that story unfolds in a sermon plot. This plot comes at the intersection of the Bible story and the particular state of the people to whom we're preaching. The plot possibilities are quite different if the congregation is made up of upwardly mobile young executives, blue-collar workers, or people with a median age of sixty-five. The narrative can follow a given character through his or her entire life. Abraham's story can unfold along the route of his altar building; Jacob is a wrestler from his mother's womb to the end of his days; Simon Peter is in conversations, negative and positive, until legend places him with the *quo vadis* question. In the same fashion, a narrative sermon can sweep through the plot of an entire book of the Bible. Exodus can be linked, in some fascinating ways, with Jean-Paul Sartre's *No Exit*. The plot is made to order, of course, in the book of Esther, or Job, or Nehemiah. Genesis gives us a phenomenal beginning ("In the beginning when God created") and ending ("in a coffin in Egypt") with events between that should enchant any storyteller.

A metaphor is also a great device for a narrative sermon. Jesus made it so each time he said, "The kingdom of heaven is like (a pearl, a treasure in a field, a bit of leaven)." His metaphor then opens possibilities for a plot. Paul tells us that the church is like a body, or our lives like a race, or holy living like garments one wears. A preacher who loves athletics finds his metaphor for the church in a team. One who preaches in a suburban executive community looks at the church in its corporate model—and rightly, if the corporation is, in fact, *corps, corpis,* a body.

The structure of a first person narrative sermon can also be very effective. As a matter of fact, it may be effective even when it's not done very well, which probably encourages some of us to try this form more often than our dramatic talents justify. A good first person portrayal allows the preacher to make some points more effectively than is possible in a straightforward presentation, and sometimes allows him or her to venture issues that would be marginal in any other form. But if you use this form, remember that you are a preacher, not an actor, and that your goal is to convey truth, not to entertain. Be properly skeptical of your dramatic abilities.

Biblical narrative sermons possess some unique strengths. Because they depend on plot, there is more likely to be an element of suspense, and of course, suspense helps maintain interest. The linear sermon tells listeners the whole story in the outline, then struggles to find anecdotes and biblical data to entice further interest, while the narrative is enticing by nature. Many truths that are nearly unpalatable in linear form can be sold in narrative. If the prophet Nathan had said to King David, "I want to give you three reasons why adultery is unacceptable behavior," I doubt that he would have gotten past his introduction.

I warn you that biblical narrative is not easy. Perhaps you have avoided it for that reason. In truth, narrative is probably no more difficult than linear, but the difficulty comes at a different time. In a biblical narrative sermon, the struggle comes at the outset, as you seek to find the plotline for that particular sermon. Once you get hold of that wondrous thread, it will likely lead you on almost beyond your will. Novelists often say that they don't know how a story is going to unfold until they see what their characters do. So, too, with a narrative sermon; frequently it carries you to places you hadn't imagined. The linear sermon, on the other hand, is quite easy at the outset. Outlines require only limited imagination, though some proper refining. Then you begin the search for illustrations, quotes, supporting material. In a narrative sermon, most of this data is implicit in the plot itself. However, the search for the plot can be disheartening, no doubt.

Some General Narrative Insights

That chief of storytellers, George Eliot, said she always feared "lapsing from the picture to a diagram." I feel that this is what many preachers do when they take a magnificent parable or Old Testament story and force it into three points. I hesitate, therefore, to suggest rules for narrative development, lest I frustrate your native, even if largely undiscovered, creative gifts. Perhaps a few insights can help the process, if they're not taken too legalistically.

First, think the passage through. The linear preacher will say, "So what else is new?" but this is a different kind of thinking. In this case, you're seeking to find what this story is about as relates to your purposes for the sermon. We preachers don't come to a sermon *tabula rasa*; we have feelings about the people to whom we'll be preaching, and about what we perceive their needs to be. We try, as much as possible, to eliminate our inclinations and prejudices, even while looking forward to what we hope to see happen in the passage through this sermon.

Second, we find the plotline. As I indicated earlier, for the preacher this plotline comes at the intersection of the text and today. This ought to be true of any good sermon, but the slant is slightly different in a narrative approach. The linear sermon may lay today and the text side by side and reflect on their combined identity; the narrative sermon brings today into a story, and in the process, unfolds a new story.

Third, the narrative sermon can begin in either the biblical story or in the present. The beginning point depends in some measure on the congregation. If the preacher ministers to people who know the Bible and love it, the sermon may well begin on this ground. With a more secular body, the preacher who begins with the Bible may for a time disguise what he's doing. So, for instance, in a sermon on King Saul, one might begin: "There's a man I've known since I was a boy in Sunday School; but knowing him as long as I have, I still haven't gotten over the tragedy of his life." I can then proceed to develop the story of Saul, and when I note that this is, indeed, a biblical character, I can explain that I was not exaggerating when I spoke of knowing him since my boyhood, because persons we come to know through history or literature become as much a part of our lives, and as real to us, as those with whom we've had face-to-face contact—as a matter of fact, sometimes more so.

Fourth, don't give away the secret, the end, or the purpose of your plot. Don't telegraph your knockout punch. Eugene Lowry, who has written as much as anyone about narrative preaching, says that the common component in narrative sermons is that "they refuse to announce a conclusion in advance."[3] There are exceptions to this rule, as there are to all rules; but as with all exceptions, you'd better know why you're making the exception.

Fifth, the plot should always relate to human need. That isn't difficult if you're preaching from the Scriptures, because human need is their primary domain. Human need has a variety of faces. It shows itself sometimes in despair, but also in pride and arrogance. There is need in the saint and in the sinner, and sometimes, if you didn't know which was which, you wouldn't guess it from the expression of the need. Need makes for poignancy in preaching, and no book reveals need in all its complexity as the Bible does. In the same vein, remember that the plot should appeal to human curiosity. Novelists and short story writers are experts at baiting readers' curiosity. The sermon plot should make us want to know what's going to happen— perhaps to the biblical story, and also to ourselves.

Remember that several possible plots await us in every biblical story. I suspect that Haddon Robinson is basically right when he urges homileticians to look for the "big idea" in a biblical passage.[4] No matter; the big idea, as it unfolds in a sermon plot, takes a different course depending on the preacher, his or her station in life, and the attributes of the congregation. Thus one can return to a given passage after a reasonable lapse of time, and it may engage a very different insight.

One further word: don't be afraid to let people make application for themselves. Fred Craddock has probably emphasized this theme more than anyone, to the benefit of hundreds of congregations. As I indicated earlier, Jesus clearly trusted his listeners more than we do. Or perhaps I should say, Jesus trusted the Holy Spirit more than we do. As I prepare to preach, I pray for the Holy Spirit to anoint my thinking and my presentation, but I also pray for the Spirit to anoint the minds and wills of those to whom I preach. It seems to me that the Spirit, plumbing the complexity of the human mind more effectively than I can, may find some areas of application that would never occur to me.

The Verse-by-Verse or Phrase-by-Phrase Sermon: The Preacher as Teacher

With verse-by-verse sermons, the preacher becomes the teacher. Mind you, we are always teaching, but this type of preaching emphasizes the teaching role. According to many popular definitions, "expository preaching" means this type of verse-by-verse work.[5] I feel that faithful narrative preaching is also expository; that is, it too unfolds the content of the text in complete fashion, but via a different style. The verse-by-verse method reveals the text by way of word study, historical and geographical background, and comparison with other portions of Scripture, while narrative method uses the medium of story.

It strikes me that two places you find this type of careful word study are in preaching, and in serious study of poetry. This kind of preaching pays high tribute to the Scriptures: it takes the text seriously. It's not surprising, then, that this type of preaching becomes especially prominent in times of church renewal, as in the Reformation. Done well, the verse-by-verse method gives listeners a depth of knowledge of the Bible. Contrary to its claims, it doesn't guarantee that the preacher will not revisit favorite themes, but it's a step in the right direction.

Shortcomings and Secrets

Verse-by-verse sermon development has built-in hazards. For one, a preacher may be inclined to limit engagement with contemporary time and culture. The preacher's fascination with the ancient text and its context can easily become an end in itself. The preacher can forget to apply the truths to the needs of the present. Indeed, sometimes the preacher becomes so intrigued with data that truth itself is quite forgotten.

This type of preaching is susceptible to authoritarianism. When one works intimately with sacred Scripture, one may begin to confuse the authority of the speaker with the authority of the document. The exegete must constantly remember that he or she is a servant of the Word. We are privileged to share our findings, and even more privileged if someone pays attention, but our authority stops there. When the preacher is a rather skilled exegete, listeners may confuse the boundary between the preacher and the document, and grant the preacher more authority than is deserved. The preacher, in turn, may conclude that the authority is merited.

There is also a danger that the preacher will give too much time to illustrative material while believing the sermon is chock full of Scripture. John S. McClure has observed that one of the finest expository preachers, Harry A. Ironside, was "less interested in careful biblical exegesis than he was in provocative application and illustration."[6] I've had the same feeling about many preachers who prided themselves on their line-by-line exposition: cut out the rather lengthy stories and what remains is a willowy creature on which no one can safely lean. As a result of doubting the interest-quality of biblical data, the preacher may be tempted to insert jokes that are sometimes only vaguely related to the subject matter. In such instances, what people tend to remember is almost always the jokes. I understand the temptation to add jokes, because line-by-line preaching can easily become tedious. The large amount of word study, geography, and ancient history may fascinate the devoted scholar, but they may lack either interest or sustenance for the person who is simply struggling to live a godly life. And to be honest, sometimes the word study and the background geography, employing, as they do, religious language, give an impression of spiritual nourishment that may not truly be there.

The biggest hazard, I feel, in even the best line-by-line exposition, is the tendency to lose the forest in the trees. It's difficult to keep a theme clearly in mind in the midst of impressive amounts of biblical information. The danger, then, is that the listener will take home a great many tidbits of knowledge, but not necessarily to any sure end. To put it in conventional terms, the sermon will be informational rather than transformational.

This problem leads us to some secrets of effective verse-by-verse preaching. First, from the outset we need to find the theme that inhabits a given passage. Having found it, we must keep aiming toward it in our preparation, and bring our sermon back to it. This means, among other things, that we won't necessarily include in the sermon every gem of word study we've unearthed. Remember, again, the principle of exclusion—"knowing what to leave out." Be sure that your material advances the theme, making it more clear, practical, and persuasive.

In the pursuit of a cohesive theme, search for the meaning in each phrase. Still better, look for the soul in each passage. When you find the insight that warms your soul, chances are good that it will warm the souls of those listening. In the process, you will also be somewhat protected against the tedium that can slip easily into line-by-line exposition. This is related to knowing what interests people—which, in most cases, has to do with where their needs lie. If we are good students of both life and Scripture, we will often unearth needs that the listener has felt but never verbalized, including perhaps some they've purposely avoided. In such instances, the impact is all the greater when the insight comes from the body of Scripture rather than more obviously from the exhortation of the preacher.

And remember when to stop. Although this is important in every kind of sermon, if I observe human nature rightly, it's more of an issue in line-by-line preaching. This type of sermon can carry a preacher along on the waves of fulfilling research. Most of us have discovered that no one bores as effectively as the person who is altogether taken with a subject that is of no interest to anyone else. But that happens almost naturally when one gets below the surface on any given subject. The preacher may not realize how long the sermon has been extended. Also, because the line-by-line sermon is not usually as artistically crafted as either the linear sermon or the narrative sermon, the conclusion may not be as structurally obvious as it ought to be. To prevent this danger, let the preacher keep a clock before the eyes, both while preparing the sermon and while preaching it.

The Sum of It All

Structurally, the preacher can develop the body of the sermon by linear, narrative, line-by-line unfolding, or any number of variations on the above! Each style has its own charm, and its own shortcomings. A preacher should probably not be taken captive by any single form, though, since I probably don't live up to this admonition, I may be a hypocrite for saying so. In any event, the preacher should know how to use each form effectively.

Know that one form will probably be more native to the preacher's temperament than the others, because most of us are inclined toward one disposition or another, whether debater, storyteller, or teacher. Perfect that form as much as you can, even while you work on other possibilities. And never succumb to thinking that your preferred form is uniquely ordained by God.

Notes

1. Dick Feagler, *Feagler's Cleveland* (Cleveland: Gray & Company, 1996), fly leaf.

2. Eugene H. Peterson, *Subversive Spirituality* (Grand Rapids, Mich.: William B. Eerdmans Pub. Co., 1997), 213.

3. Eugene Lowry, *The Sermon* (Nashville: Abingdon Press, 2001), 28.

4. Haddon W. Robinson, *Biblical Preaching: The Development and Delivery of Expository Messages,* 2d ed. (Grand Rapids, Mich.: Baker Academic, 2001).

5. William H. Willimon and Richard Lischer, eds. *Concise Encyclopedia of Preaching* (Louisville: Westminster John Knox Press, 1995), 131.

6. John S. McClure, "Expository Preaching" *Concise Encyclopedia of Preaching*, 132.

CHAPTER SEVEN

The Dotted Line

In truth, the sermon exists for its conclusion. This is an existential difference between a lecture and a sermon. From the beginning, the aim of a sermon is to get to a place where the listener wants to do something about the subject we've presented: this is the moment of the dotted line. That is, every sermon, by definition, ought to be evangelistic. I use the term broadly, but without apology. You and I are preaching in the most evangelistic age in human history; why should we be embarrassed that we, too, are evangelists? Indeed, if we are not, what is our case for existence? We can't be content simply to convey information, any more than we would be content to be the court jester.

When I speak of ours being the most evangelistic age in human history, I'm not speaking about television evangelists or media campaigns or Billy Graham and his successors. I suspect the best term is the one Paul Tillich gave us when he described religion as the state of "ultimate concern."[1] We humans are all but deluged with concerns, but only one is ultimate; only one gives significance and value to the very fact of our being.

But we are being evangelized constantly to accept some secondary concern—or far, far less than that—as if it were our ultimate concern. The appeal is subtle, because it rarely asks us directly to claim one of these lesser concerns as our salvation. But let these lesser concerns go to work on us, and eventually, in their Lilliputian way, they will bind us to earth. This is a dreadful conclusion for creatures like you and me, who are impregnated with eternity.

The secular evangelists are constantly, unceasingly at work. A major New York advertising executive said a few years ago that the "average 50-year-old has had an estimated 5,000 advertising messages thrown at him or her every day of his or her life. Between the time you wake up in the morning and the time you get to work, you're bombarded with come-ons."[2] The newspaper, radio, television, billboards, store displays, signs on the shopping cart, ads even in the restaurant restroom. By the best estimate, in the year 2000, some two hundred billion dollars was spent in America on advertising. Essentially, these billions of dollars were spent to convince us that Jesus was wrong when he said, "one's life does not consist in the abundance of possessions." Blaise Pascal said that there is in every person a God-shaped void that only God can fill. A materialistic culture says, "Let's see if we can fill it."

Now let me be clear. These secular evangelists haven't announced that they are after our souls. Many of them would be amused by the very concept. They're after our glands, our gullets, our minds, our psyches, and our wallets. And getting these, they will almost surely get our souls by default, without our even knowing that it has happened.

It seems that the game is played on a very uneven field. The people to whom you and I preach once a week have been seduced and evangelized all through the week by literally thousands of appeals. And those appeals have come from some of the most creative minds in our culture, backed by almost obscene budgets. As it happens, however, you and I have a hidden advantage. We have the only product (if I may use that term) that ultimately satisfies the human soul, because we deal exclusively in the ultimate. But our advantage is diminished, and sometimes even lost, if we fail to bring persons to the dotted line.

The Nature of Decision

Our dotted line is more than simply accepting Jesus Christ as Lord and Savior. This kind of preaching has turned the rushing torrents of the gospel into a very shallow, and sometimes stagnant pool. Yes, the Lordship of Christ is the ultimate issue, but this Lordship is spelled out in the unending decisions of daily life: family, work, sports, entertainment, investments, food, drink, clothing, sex, music, politics, citizenship, reading, listening, talking, giving, spending. If we are to live eternally in a culture that is stiflingly secular and material, we will need a process of eternal evangelizing, because God and hell know that we're being constantly evangelized the other way.

The conclusion ought to make some decision accessible and impelling. While every sermon surely ought to inform, it doesn't qualify as a sermon unless it also seeks to transform. Sometimes the transformation is so monumental that the person recalls it ever after, sometimes using the classic term "born again." But it is also a conversion when a person leaves church resolving to be a better spouse or parent, or when giving increases from nominal to significant, or when morality and ethics are realized to be more important in politics than Democratism or Republicanism. Indeed, it is a magnificent sermon when a depressed human being sees new reason to go on living, or a self-despising soul smiles at his own image. Our pulpit ancestors in the American tradition probably did a better job with conclusions. Perhaps it was part of our frontier tradition, with its sense of peril on the one hand, and of new beginnings on the other. Action was called for in either event. I suspect we also lost some of our "dotted-line sense" during the religious controversies that tended to equate evangelism with fundamentalism. Then, worse, there was a period in the 1970s and early 1980s when many in the mainline pulpit gloried in saying, "My job is to raise questions, not to provide answers." With such a mind-set, the dotted line is hardly a compelling possibility.

Truthfully, the conclusion is difficult under any circumstances. Only a coach at half-time in a locker room finds it easy to go from "Here's what's wrong with us" to "Now let's go out and win!" One needs an analytical mind, a subtle level of psychological insight, and an intense, focused passion to do it well. Because a good conclusion is logical and intelligent, it exhibits an understanding of the audience, and it has a sensitive expression of emotion.

The conclusion ought to be relatively brief. There are exceptions, of course, depending on the nature of the sermon. Some linear sermons may call for a fairly long summary, or the conclusion may be made with a relatively long but effective illustration. As a rule, the conclusion is not a place for amplification—that should have happened in the body. It's probably too late to redeem things in the conclusion if it hasn't. It's painful for a preacher to realize this, however, when he or she suddenly feels that something should have been made more clear or more compelling at an earlier point.

Don't signal that the end is coming. When the preacher says, "I close with this," he or she generally should have closed some minutes earlier. As soon as you say something like, "Now, in conclusion," or "Just one more thing," you have divided the listener's focus. Instead of concentrating on what you're saying, they begin to think of what they're going to do when the sermon ends. Even at best, that's always a siren voice in the listener's ear, and we shouldn't do anything to facilitate it. And especially, avoid a two-minute warning. Your estimate and the listener's estimate of the time remaining will almost surely be different—to your disadvantage.

For those familiar with our preaching, we may give signals of the approaching close without our knowing it. As a frequent flyer, I pay little attention to landing time unless

I'm making a close connection. But I do recognize, instinctively, when a plane goes into a holding pattern. Your frequent listeners often develop the same sense. They know that your homiletical plane ought to land, and they wonder what's gone wrong in the control room that you're still circling the airport.

Forms of Conclusion

The linear sermon often concludes, appropriately, with a summary. If the outline is important, as implied in a linear sermon, then the conclusion should probably not forget its importance. You have three points, or however many, because you feel the idea is best delivered in this fashion. Reaffirm those points, and if necessary, redefine each one with a sentence, but no more.

Often a concluding summary in a linear sermon needs help from another source. The great Scottish preacher James Stuart Stewart often turned to a poem. I suspect that if one is eloquent, has the poem well in control, and knows how to deliver, that type of conclusion can still be effective. But this is a lot of *if*. African American preachers can often find power in the quoting of a familiar hymn; when I do so, it's a pretty ordinary experience for the congregation.

One of the most popular forms of conclusion is the story or illustration. Done well, it is exceedingly moving; as a result, too many preachers try it, and do it poorly. The fault is not with the method, but with our carelessness in employing it. This is at least partly because too many preachers get their illustrations from a volume of nice stories or from the Internet. Sometimes the closing story fails to move the audience, which is a painful experience for the preacher. Sometimes it moves the audience, but it doesn't move them toward where the sermon was going because it isn't integrally related to the sermon. This second situation doesn't pain the preacher as deeply, but it ought to, because it means that most of what was said in the body of the sermon has now been scuttled by the conclusion.

I'm impressed that so many of Harry Emerson Fosdick's sermons ended with a story, for example, one about Andrew Melville, an early Scotch reformer, with three powerful sentences from Melville. Some who feel that nothing said before 2001 is interesting will complain that no one knows who Andrew Melville was. No matter! If the story is powerful, you will want ever after to know more about him. Fosdick told a story that was only a few weeks old at the time, after the good ship *Gripsholm* had returned with a group of missionaries released from a Japanese concentration camp. Time was then on Fosdick's side, but I find the story still moving me half a century later. Another sermon ends with an excerpt from Lord Shaftesbury's diary, concerning his battle in Parliament for the poor. Again, Fosdick made use of three short sentences, well chosen and powerful.

In all of these stories, Dr. Fosdick wasted not a word. He usually tells the story in one brief paragraph. Most preachers succumb to poor preparation or to a love affair with detail, and the story drags when it should soar. Find the right story—right for your sermon, for your congregation, and for your personality—and keep it brief.

When we were discussing introductions, I suggested the rule, "Let the dog swallow its tail." When you keep this idea in mind, your conclusion is already half-made, because it has its essence in your introduction and in your title. John Gardner, the twentieth century American novelist and poet, said "a novel is like a symphony in that its closing movement echoes and resounds with all that has gone before."[3] So it is with the sermon. Peter Marshall, chaplain to the U.S. Senate in the mid-twentieth century, titled a sermon "The Art of Moving Mountains." He began with the observation that most of us have seen the motto, "Prayer changes things," then moved, within the opening minute, to his text, Matthew 17:20, in which Jesus promises that faith can move mountains. He presented the subject with a variety of materials over the next little while, then came back to his title and introduction with these closing lines: "Try a little mountain-moving . . . and you will find it the greatest adventure of your life."[4] A novelist couldn't have done it better.

The conclusion that finds its theme in the title and introduction blesses both the preacher and the listener. For the preacher, it simplifies the search for closing material by narrowing the field. For the listener, it makes the sermon more compact, more focused, and thus easier to remember.

Another way to conclude is to find something personal in yourself, as preacher, or in your hearers. Charles Williams, the novelist who was part of "The Inklings" along with C. S. Lewis and J. R. R. Tolkien, was said to be almost as good a lecturer as a novelist. Why? Because during the discussion period following his lectures he "electrified his audience into believing that they themselves were almost as clever and interesting as he was."[5] The preacher needs something of this electrifying skill, so that the listeners will feel the degree to which the preacher believes in them, and cares about their welfare. Part of the secret is simply to care that much. But it's also a matter of communicating this caring. I've known many a loving pastor whose audiences never grasped how much they were loved. This is why the conclusion should have a very personal quality, either from what the preacher reveals about himself or herself, or because the listeners are made to feel significant. Arthur Miller, perhaps the greatest playwright of the twentieth century, was asked to explain the difference between an ordinary play and a great drama. He answered, "In any successful play, there must be something which makes the audience say to themselves, 'Good Lord, that's me! That's me!' "[6]

However, sometimes a forthright telling that the sermon is about the listener causes the listener to raise a barrier: "You're not going to tell me who I am." The feeling of identifying with a sermon has to come through the passion of the preacher and the vistas of humanity that the sermon has revealed. Sometimes this comes best when the preacher reveals himself or herself. When the preacher says, honestly and unaffectedly, "If you wonder by what authority I have preached this sermon, it is because I have traveled this road. And I confess I haven't always traveled it well. But I know the road, and know that in it I have found the grace of God. So it is that I dare to speak it to you."

Soul in the Conclusion

In a lecture at The Yale School of Drama, "Black Preaching as an Art Form," Dr. Earl F. Miller recalled a conversation with Dr. Miles Jones. "Earl," Jones said, "in black preaching, if when you get through, your people don't feel like getting up and doing something, then you haven't preached." I couldn't agree more. Soul is the issue in all of preaching, but never more so than in the sermon's conclusion. By its nature, soul demands response. Soul isn't content to convey information, to impress, or to amuse. Soul insists on being engaged with the holy. After delivering his or her soul, the preacher passionately wants a response from the souls of the hearers. I remember a young evangelist a long generation ago who said, "I don't care if you argue with me, resent me, or get angry with me; just don't ignore me." That's soul.

Soul makes its way all through the sermon, aiming toward the dotted line. The charm of the introduction and the well-chosen material of the body exist for the sake of the conclusion. How unfortunate, then, if we do our conclusions poorly! Why all the prior effort if we can't reach the dotted line?

Notes

1. Daniel G. Reid, ed. *Dictionary of Christianity in America* (Downers Grove, Ill.: InterVarsity Press, 1990), 1175-6.

2. Jerry Della Femina, "When Will Madison Avenue Get It?" *New York Times Magazine* 14b, no. 50726 (1997): 74.

3. John Gardner, *The Art of Fiction: Notes on Craft for Young Writers* (New York: Vintage Books, 1985), 184.

4. Peter Marshall, *John Doe, Disciple* (New York: McGraw-Hill, 1963), 173, 185.

5. Humphrey Carpenter, *The Inklings* (Boston: Houghton Mifflin, 1978), 101.

6. William J. Bausch, *Storytelling the Word* (Mystic, Conn.: Twenty-Third Publications, 1996), 40.

CHAPTER EIGHT

Don't Strip-Mine a Text

The Creator may have invested as much raw, natural beauty in the rugged hills of America's Appalachian Mountains as can be found anywhere on earth. But there's gold in many of those hills, the black gold of coal, and impatient greed has scorned the beauty of the hills while seeking their wealth. The temptation is particularly great when seams of coal lie relatively near the surface of the earth. Then the huge earth-moving equipment scoops away the top layer of rock and earth that covers the coal. Unless great care is taken, strip-mining not only destroys the beauty that nature has taken aeons to develop, but also it often leaves the land open to erosion and depletion. If hundreds of mining operations have strip-mined the hills of the coal country, thousands of preachers do similar violence week after week to the texts entrusted to their care. I don't know enough about mining to say how many veins of coal are left below the surface when the strip miners have done their work. But I've listened to preaching for as long as I can remember, and I'm utterly sure that those who strip-mine a text generally leave untouched the most rewarding veins of insight. They forge through some top layer of language and culture, then take the most obvious insights from the chosen pericope and leave the rich potential of the passage untouched, though perhaps spoiled for any future homiletical effort. However rich the material that lies on the surface of the text, that which is beneath is far richer.

Those who listened to Jesus said that he "spoke with authority, unlike the scribes to whom they were accustomed." Many elements went into that authority. I dare to say that one factor was Jesus' insistence on going below the surface of a text. Much of the Sermon on the Mount is nothing more than taking traditional teachings to a deeper vein of meaning. "You have heard that it was said to those of ancient times, 'You shall not murder.'" Then Jesus went several steps deeper: if you get angry with another, if you insult them, if you call them fools (Matthew 5:21-23). I see persons who had always comfortably applied this commandment to others now recognize that it applies to them. So, too, with adultery, divorce, and retaliation; suddenly these matters were no longer issues to be applied to the outskirts of humanity, but issues of their own conduct and of their relationship with God.

Nobel Laureate Albert Szent-Györgyi said "Discovery is seeing what everybody else has seen, then thinking what nobody else has thought." This is true whether one's sought-after discovery is in physics, nuclear chemistry, economics, or next Sunday's sermon. I respect the importance of working, whenever possible, with the original biblical languages, but the issue here is not one's skill with Greek and Hebrew; it is one's willingness to sit patiently before a passage, turn it from side to side, imagine it from the varieties of human experience, and to love it passionately. Then—in what seems at times to be almost miraculous—a familiar phrase blazes with meaning.

Now and again a thoughtful student raises this question: "The basic idea in a text can be stated in just a few minutes; how do you fill 18 or 25 minutes—or even ten or twelve minutes—without resorting simply to filler?" When I hear that question I become almost despondent at the thought of those congregations where most of what they hear, week after week, is filler. Too often the preacher's inclination is to fill the sermon's appointed time with an illustration, a poem, a joke, or several quotes; or quite frequently, to seek out a variety of supporting Scriptures, all of which they can then strip-mine in the same ruthless fashion as their text. The secret is to go deeper, not broader. Thrust yourself into the very blood and sinew of the passage. What is its background? If you know the likely author of the portion, does this passage reflect something unique from the writer's life? If you don't know the author, what does this passage tell you about his or her psyche? I don't know who wrote, "Turn away the disgrace that I dread, for your ordinances are good" (Psalm 119:39), but I know this writer is my kin, because I too draw back from disgrace. After a lifetime of reading the Bible, I am convinced that there is no novel, poetry, drama, or collection of essays that reveal so tellingly the depths of the human experience. How dare we be satisfied to pluck from it some pallid admonition.

When a sermon treats the Scripture text superficially, it will most likely also treat life superficially. If we strip-mine the Scripture, we will also strip-mine human experience. Jorie Graham, one of our finer contemporary poets, says that "reading is not something we learn well in most high schools in this country any more," because reading isn't "about being able to read the surface and repeat the content. It involves being able to undergo the experience that the writer has undergone in the poem."[1] The preacher seeks to undergo the experience of both the biblical writer and of the persons to whom the sermon will be addressed. We seek to enter into both of these great veins of living: the life reflected in the Scripture passage and the life that is being experienced by our congregation. If we enter well, we find depths in both places that will make our preaching wonderfully more relevant.

When travelers to England marvel at its breathtaking gardens, they're likely to hear about Capability Brown, the legendary landscape architect. He was famous for exclaiming, as he looked at a garden or an estate, that he saw great capabilities there. I wish that his tribe would increase among us preachers. Each pericope has such enchanting capabilities; how sad if we settle for what has always been said, then try to pretty it up by a remotely related illustration!

To do so not only robs the Scripture passage entrusted to our care, but also the persons who listen to us. Thoughtful laypeople so often complain that the preaching they hear lacks seriousness. If that is true, we are insulting both our people and our sacred text, because we aren't treating either one seriously.

What We Can Do About It

Many preachers will say, sometimes with real pain, that they simply aren't able to find more in the text. They will explain that they take every minute possible, between their administrative and pastoral tasks, to prepare their sermons, but that they don't have the time for extensive research. I empathize. For nearly forty years, I did my week-by-week preaching under just such circumstances. But I also know that these constraints of the pastoral life are not all liabilities. Pastoral relationships are the very stuff that keep us real. When we listen to people's joys and pains, we are often in the territory from which the book of Psalms came. When they complain of the injustices they meet in the work place, or the disgust awakened within the political process, they may not be far from the mood of the Old Testament prophets. Listen well; the message may be an ancient Hebrew one, even if the accent is American. Those pastors who say that they cannot preach under several hundred calls a year reflect the intimacy and the contemporaneousness that come to preaching when we listen well to the voices of those to whom we minister.

Use more reading time for novels and poetry, memoirs and biographies. It's often said that poets are the guardians of our language; they are also often the most sensitive diagnosticians of the soul. Thoughtful reading outside the specific world of religion will enlarge a preacher's sympathies. Often we find that those who are outside our specific area are not as removed from us as we might think. Particularly, writers often help a preacher to read the Bible with new eyes, and that's what we need.

When it comes to the sermon process itself, *plan ahead*. If our first thought of next Sunday's sermon comes on Monday morning (or worse yet, Thursday or Friday morning), there will be little chance for the kind of searching study that a sermon deserves. No wonder, then, if we resort to strip-mining! However, if we're always planning some weeks ahead, so that we know in early March what we will be preaching about in mid-April, our unconscious mind will work small wonders for us. The fleeting thoughts that come in March, while we're working on other sermons, may not in themselves seem terribly substantial, but they provide the creative complex for deeper thinking in April's preparation. I've found the subconscious mind to be one of my best allies. I consider it particularly hospitable to the work of the Holy Spirit. But the subconscious can't be expected to work *ex nihilo*. We must give it some soil in which the soul can germinate.

It's true that we preachers don't have enough time to think. We're far too rushed, even if we are not always as productive as we should be. But there are many settings where the mind can be productive if only we intentionally claim them. This is especially true of the time we spend in the automobile. Direct your mind at such times. Get into your car with a Scripture passage in mind. Our time in the automobile is often the most private in the whole day. Don't waste it in idle thought, or worse yet, in worry, frustration, or self-pity.

When you get to your desk, don't be in too much of a hurry to look into the commentaries. Immerse your soul in the soul of the text until the two are at home with each other. Read and listen until you catch the heartbeat of the passage. This may or may not be the literary core or theme of the passage; you're looking, rather, for that quality in the passage that speaks uniquely to your soul—which is usually a pretty good indication that you will be able to communicate it to the souls of others. Mind you, I'm not by any means giving license to play fast and loose with the text. Quite the contrary. I want you to get into the text all the way, down below the obvious and the predictable. Be particularly sensitive to the human feeling of the passage. The Scriptures have a unique vitality; to present them dispassionately is a kind of subtle heresy. To be true to the Scriptures we must be true to their spirit as well as to their letter.

The Scriptures are sometimes a lush valley, sometimes great hills, sometimes mountains so stark as to be foreboding. But whatever their surface beauty, as we go deeper, they are increasingly rich. Edmund Wilson, one of the best literary critics of the twentieth century, once said that novels may commit every sin except the unpardonable one: "It does not fail to live." I can put up with a good many failings in a sermon, if only it lives—if only it gets far enough below the surface to honor its sacredness and to regard the intelligence and hunger of the listener. We shouldn't settle for less, and we shouldn't impose less on the people who trust us with a piece of their time each week.

Note

1. Craig Lambert, "Image and the Arc of Feeling," *Harvard Magazine* 103, no. 3 (2001): 41.

CHAPTER NINE

Wood, Hay, Stubble, and Precious Stones

So the preacher has what promises to be a scintillating idea, a plan or an outline of admirable symmetry, and an insight that is firmly grounded in Scripture. Now what? Now comes the process of building a sermon. Because all we have so far are blueprints, and as promising as they may be, you can't move into them. You need the stuff that makes the blueprints a habitable structure. A great many preachers begin compiling and constructing materials before their blueprint has any substantial form. They have a choice illustration, a good quote, and maybe a little biblical research, and with these they begin building without any sure knowledge as to what the finished edifice might look like. They not only raise up a ramshackle building with such a method, but also they waste wonderful material that would otherwise stir the soul in a different project.

Words, Words, Words

Let's begin with the smallest, most elemental, and most crucial of our materials, our language. It is a sacred trust. If there is anything, other than our reach toward God, about us human beings that is touched by the divine, it is our use of language. Fragile as words are (hardly more than a breath or a jot and a tittle) they are the most powerful instrument entrusted to us human beings. Atomic and hydrogen bombs may threaten our civilization, but it is words that will determine whether or not those bombs are used. Materialism endangers our very souls, but it is the artful words of the advertisers that stimulates materialism into action. Whether for good or ill, words control and empower us. As Eugene Peterson has said, "A word is (or can be) a revelation from one interior to another. What is inside me can get inside you—the word does it."[1]

But words have their seasons, as do all matters related to us human beings. I believe words were at their best in the days of Shakespeare and of the King James Bible. Now they face a struggle. It's partly a matter of our hurried lifestyle; good language takes time. It's also a result of the insistent prominence of visual imagery. As a novelist, E. L. Doctorow no doubt speaks with some prejudice, but it's hard to refute his comments in *City of God* when he insists that "the term *film language* is an oxymoron." He reminds us that language *thinks*, because it "flowers to thought with nouns, verbs, objects," but that because film is "time-driven, it never ruminates, it shows the outside of life. . . . It tends to the simplest moral reasoning."[2]

Language is also in retreat on the stage. There it once carried the day, with setting and movement providing the context. Today it more often is lost, either in shock-language, which is almost no language at all, or in quirkiness or cleverness of plot, of characters, or of stagecraft. The point is best demonstrated in musicals. Once we went away from a musical singing snatches (sometimes whole verses) of "Some Enchanted Evening," "Dream the Impossible Dream," or "With a Little Bit of Luck." Current musicals, like *Phantom of the Opera* or *Beauty and the Beast* send us home in awe of a spectacle, but with rarely a tune, and almost never a lyric. I'm not discrediting the genius that goes into such spectacular shows; I'm only insisting that the role of language has been greatly diminished.

But here's an irony. When you try, after the show, to tell friends or coworkers about it, you have to resort to language to convey what you saw, heard, and experienced. The necessity for language is inescapable. The problem for the preacher, therefore, is not to find substitutes for language, but to perfect the rendering of the magnificent gift of words.

If poets are the keepers of written language, I think a case can be made that we preachers are the keepers of spoken language. Television newscasters probably speak to more people each week, but only in utilitarian language. The preacher, too, uses utilitarian language, because part of our task is to convey information. But our utilitarian language is to the end of persuasion, inspiration, and transformation. We deal in the language of the heart. For this reason, the preacher's use of language is wonderfully complicated. We deal often in scholarly matters; indeed, we're supposed to be scholars in biblical studies, theology, ethics, and perhaps a few other matters as well. However, we must vigorously resist the use of scholarly language in our preaching, because our task is to interpret these matters to persons whose expertise is in very different fields. The scholarly language of our field is unknown to them and always has a quality of sterility about it: preaching must have soul.

We seek to become masters of language, and masters in a fashion more challenging than in any other field. Our language can't be too pretty, or we lose immediacy and power. It dare not be too technical, because our business is everyday, every-hour business. It must have clarity, without seeming pedestrian. And it should be beautiful. Several years ago Christ Otto, one of my students, wrote in a term paper that "not many preachers are known for memorable quotes or striking images." He pleaded for preachers to rediscover the possibility of making the message "an art form." It's necessary, he said, "for the sake of our culture" for the preacher "to rise above this wasteland of communication and still communicate." If we preachers believe that God is a communicator, and that Christ is the Word, then we, of all people, ought to have a high regard for language, and ought to work passionately, not only to find the best possible conveyers of our message, but also to feel that we have a stake in the very fact of language.

The Discreet Use of Windows

Preachers seem always to be on a stretch and a strain to find sermon illustrations. At a lecture for a clergy event, you see the pens come out and the desktops activate if you tell a story that might somehow fit into a sermon. I regret that many sermon illustrations sound as if they have been dragged in as filler, or that they are used to relieve tacitly confessed tedium in the biblical exposition.

As commonly used, illustrations are greatly overrated; if preachers were policed professionally, many would be barred for malpractice of illustrative material. One of the most heinous crimes is the use of someone else's personal illustration as if it were your own story. I would not believe this were possible if I hadn't seen it happen so many times. Barbara Brown Taylor, whose recent Beecher Lectures on preaching were particularly notable, tells of a friend who said, "I wish someone would tell preachers not to lie. It is better to tell your own pitiful story, whatever that may be, than to puff it up by lying." This includes, Dr. Taylor says, "passing other people's language off as your own."[3]

Teachers of preaching have long described illustrations as "windows" in the sermon. It's a proper term; a good illustration sheds light on the subject. But if a house has too many windows, the windows cease to serve their purpose and become a distraction. The preacher must be very sure that the illustration does, indeed, illustrate the subject at hand. It shouldn't be simply an attention-getter, or relief from the tedium of heavier material. It must advance the point, or make it more accessible. Otherwise, the illustration is likely to distract from the sermon by encouraging the listener to attend to something other than what the sermon is about. For that reason, there is no such thing as a good illustration in isolation. It's a good illustration only as it illustrates. Standing alone, it's a story; when it throws light on something, it's an illustration. And when it throws light on the right thing, the appropriate thing, then it's a *good* illustration. The worth of an illustration is in how it is put to work.

Where are good illustrations to be found? They are almost everywhere, though rarely in books of illustrations and the Internet. Truly good illustrations almost always lay some sort of claim on the preacher; they find the preacher more often than the preacher finds them. The problem is that good illustrations don't necessarily find us when we're in need of them. That's why we need to give them a home when they come our way, so they'll be around when we need them.

The best illustrations are often embedded in the passage from which we're preaching. As we examine its depths, stories appear, insights on human nature strike, and perceptions of the eternal capture us. And of course, the illustrations for a given pericope may come from the background of the passage, especially in the story of the biblical character.

Stories are everywhere where human life is lived, explained, recalled, laughed at, and sung about. The secret is to expose ourselves to the human condition. When Irwin Shaw, the American novelist and playwright, was young and finding his way, he got an interesting insight from Somerset Maugham, who was then at his peak. Maugham told Shaw that he envied him. Shaw thought Maugham was being ironic, but replied, "Why do you envy me, Mr.

Maugham?" Maugham replied, "Because you are an American and write short stories. There is a short story on every street corner in America. I have to go through a whole country to find one."[4] On every corner, indeed. I find stories in the airport, in the fast food restaurant's line, as I wait my turn at the hotel desk, or stand on the corner in a small town. Artists in other fields train their senses better than many of us do. Ingmar Bergman, the Swedish film genius, said that he would sometimes follow an intoxicated man down the street at night, just to see the way he put his feet, so he could replicate it faithfully in a film. I don't recommend such emotional detachment to the preacher, but I do recommend the intensity of observation employed by the better film makers, novelists, and poets.

Novels can be a source of illustrations, as long as you don't feel obligated to summarize the whole story in order to reach your thirty-second incident. It seems almost impossible to use an illustration from a movie without going into tedious background detail. Poetry can be a rich source; is there any better story anywhere than Edwin Arlington Robinson has left us in "Richard Cory" or "Miniver Cheevy"? And Edgar Lee Masters's old classic *Spoon River Anthology* has so many penetrating portraits that a preacher would do well to revisit it every several years.

The speaker who handles historical material without going into too many details will find that it still provides some of the best illustrative material. And while using it, the preacher may deliver some people from their neurotic fixation with the present. Biography and autobiography are also abundant in illustrations. I find that the best are often those biographies that concentrate on the subject's interior world. *The Little Locksmith* by Katharine Butler Hathaway, was once hard to come by, except in libraries that hadn't become fanatical about winnowing out old books, but has recently been republished and offers handfuls of anecdotes and insights.

Never go far without a handheld tape recorder when you travel, so you can record what you find on obscure historical markers and in the halls of state capitols. And don't think you have to wait until you can go to the Holy Land, or England, or the sites of the Reformation. Henry David Thoreau said, "I have travelled a good deal in Concord." (Funny; I've often heard that quoted "and Lexington," as if we couldn't be content that for Thoreau, Concord was enough.) The secret is seeing what we're looking at. James A. Michener, who's done a bit of writing himself, says that great writers "are people like Emily Brontë who write out of limited experience and unlimited imagination." It's not a matter of how widely we've traveled this earth, nor the stature of the people we've met, but a matter of our being sensitive to what we see and hear, so that it becomes the stuff of the soul.

What We Shall Say About Ourselves

How often, and in what ways, shall preachers use themselves as the source of sermon material? The question is difficult because few things are more persuasive than one's own witness, yet few things are more easily abused.

The two most serious abuses are exaggeration and self-aggrandizement. I don't know why it is, but preachers seem particularly susceptible to exaggeration. Nowhere is this worse than in the recounting of experiences: ordinary events become monumental; passing acquaintances are "dear friends"; a form acknowledgment from a celebrity becomes "our years of correspondence." Those stories do more to glamorize the preacher than to advance a point. The preacher must search his or her heart to be sure, first of all, that the story is true in all its details; and second, that it is being used for the right reasons, and third, that one is not introducing elements that will subtly turn the spotlight on oneself.

Those precautions having been taken, it must be said that personal illustrations have inherent soul. They are you, and they are more able to speak to others. The practice of personal illustrations is also biblical. Jeremiah's prophecies are full of his own pain. The passage from Isaiah that is probably most quoted is the most self-revealing one: "In the year that King Uzziah died, I saw the Lord" (Isaiah 6:1). Paul's letters are jam-packed with personal expressions of joy, regret, hurt, and defensiveness.

I'm not speaking of the sometimes-popular practice of "pouring out your guts" for an audience. That is not self-revealing, but exhibitionistic, and exhibitionists are never truly revealing because they're too absorbed with portraying a particular image of themselves. When we share who we are, how we have laughed and have cried, when we share both the pain of our failures and the exhilarations of our successes, we give a unique authenticity to our message. And sometimes we do so without any specific reference to our story; the hearer is left to infer it. In any event, there should be restraint.

Arthur John Gossip magnificently demonstrated his authenticity without elaborating on his personal feelings in the first sermon he preached after his wife's "dramatically sudden" death, "But When Life Tumbles in, What Then?" He says nothing of the degree of his pain, no attempts at heart-rending details. His personal observations are as muted as his statement midway, "I don't think that anyone will challenge my right to speak today."[5] Yet his experience is a compelling undercurrent throughout the sermon, from title to closing sentence. Nor should we ever feel our experience is too commonplace to have any merit. After B. B. King sang for the Nieman Fellows at Harvard some years ago, he opened himself for an interview by that select group of journalists. He said that growing up in the Delta doesn't give one a monopoly on the blues. "You don't have to be poor to understand resentment or disloyalty, to be misused or unloved. You don't have to be poor or black. Like when Rockefeller was running for president—he had the blues. Anybody can sing the blues."[6]

In some instances, we might do well to follow the style of the apostle Paul. When it came to a matter of boasting about visions and revelations, he chose to use the third person: "I know a person in Christ who fourteen years ago . . ." (2 Corinthians 12:2). We may choose for matters of personal privacy, or in order to preserve some shreds of humility, to cast a personal story as "I knew a person once who . . . " Don't be afraid to use personal references, because few arrows in the preacher's quiver more surely originate from his or her soul and go directly to the soul of the listener. Be constantly cautious of your integrity and of your motives.

Statistics and Quotes

The preacher will employ statistics from time to time in a culture where one can get a doctorate in statistics, politicians get daily numerical reports on public opinion, and nearly every periodical has a box somewhere with some figures to surprise the reader. Fair enough, but keep some rules in mind.

Perhaps the best rule is implicit in the words of Benjamin Disraeli, a prime minister of Great Britain in the late nineteenth century: "There are three kinds of lies: lies, damned lies, and statistics." People too quickly say, "Well, the numbers are right here; it's a fact." Statistics are easily twisted, both in the way they're compiled and in the way they're used. We can govern the way they're used, and we'd better do so if we have any integrity. We can't control the way they've been compiled, so we have to depend on the integrity of our sources. We can also learn, in some instances, something about the way the data has been collected, or the kinds of questions used in the course of a public opinion poll. One sometimes hears statistics in a sermon that are patently open to question. Such statistics not only do not advance a point; for a critical listener, they may undermine the entire sermon. Statistics are easily overdone. One good statistic is impressive. Two can be convincing. Three can bring a glaze to the eyes and indifference to the mind. When we pile evidence on evidence, we're likely to trivialize the whole collection.

Quotes are valuable, basically, for two reasons: as a source of authority, and for flavor. Preachers seem to quote primarily for authority. Thus the phrase, "Now, the Bible says . . . " But we also quote theologians, scholars, historical personalities, political figures, and in this celebrity-crazed day, entertainers and athletes. One must be sure, in quoting for authority, that the person quoted is, indeed, an authority. This is both an objective and a subjective matter. No matter how good a person's credentials objectively, their words won't help much unless they carry authority with the hearer. On the whole, an authority is an authority only in his or her own field, but in the case of religious experience the rule no longer applies. As the late Roy L. Smith said a generation ago, "The person who has an experience with God has something beyond the reach of any argument." A person need not be a Bible scholar or a philosopher to speak of their personal faith in God. On the other hand, in certain circles the philosopher who makes such a witness is more effective than just anyone.

The quote for flavor generally has nothing to do with authority; it's a matter of beauty. This is the quote we use because it can't be said better. Such quotes rarely come from professional scholars, but from novelists, poets, playwrights, comic strips, and country-western music. And, if I may say it without offense, from simple folk: from persons whose speech hasn't been "trained" to the point of losing its original nuances. You know someone like this: an aged relative, a quirky aunt, a taciturn farmer. Three baseball players have become almost better known for their quotes than for their athletics: Casey Stengel, Satchel Paige, and Yogi Berra. Whether a quote is used for authority or for flavor, keep it brief. Very brief. The eminent Civil War historian, William Best Hesseltine, used to insist that anything beyond six words should go into the footnotes. Longer quotes often indicate that the preacher has turned lazy; it's easier to quote someone than to put the material into one's own words. And as most of us would confess, it's doubtful that we understand something unless we can put it into our own words. Every speaker has her or his own rhythm. If we quote someone else for even a solid paragraph, we lose our rhythm, our identity, and our soul—and in the process, the hearer's attention.

Students sometimes say they dare not quote from a poet or a novelist because their people won't recognize the person or the work. Nonsense. In truth, in our exceedingly diverse society there's no reference that can be made beyond three standard political quotes that will be recognized by everyone. The preacher need only offer a basis for mental location: "the nineteenth century poet," or "the World War II newspaper correspondent." If the quote is a good one, it will carry itself pretty well, and if it requires too much outside bolstering, it's not worth using. Remember, too, that a side benefit of good preaching ought to be an enlarging of our listeners' minds. This is only a secondary matter, but a worthy one. And incidentally, if a reference you make—to a movie, a novel, or a television show—is recognized by everyone in your congregation, your congregation is seriously segregated. Not by race or ethnicity, but by lifestyle. You need to start integrating it, for your sake and theirs.

Then, There's the Bible

I leave the Bible last, not because it is least important, but to the contrary, because I consider it a given. I doubt that a sermon can be called Christian without a thorough immersion in Scripture. I'm not speaking of chapter-and-verse quoting, and certainly not of proof-texting, but of the simple fact that the Bible is our basic document. Without it, we are bereft. And while it is true that some say they are "turned off" by the Bible, they usually mean that they are turned off by a certain kind of Bible usage. It's our job to show them a better way.

Our use of the Bible in preaching should be marked by solid scholarship, but not conspicuously so. Preachers sometimes undercut the priesthood of believers by their handling of the Bible. If the person in the pew is unduly impressed by our scholarship, it may mean that we are parading it. I think I need not tell you that this is not a good thing. A nineteenth century Scottish preacher commented dryly as he concluded the reading of the morning lesson, "If Shakespeare had said that, we should never have heard the end of it." The same words might well be spoken about any number of pundits and personalities in our day.

The Sum of It All

The material we put into our sermon must, in the end, be the very stuff of eternity, because that's the nature of our business. Some works, the apostle Paul said, are wood, hay, and stubble, and will be consumed at the judgment, while others will stand the test because they are gold, silver, and precious stones. As we choose the material that goes into the sermon, let us always choose broadly enough that reasonable persons of every age and lifestyle can hear us, but let us aim high enough that we accomplish the purpose of our calling, which is eternal.

Notes

1. Eugene H. Peterson, *Subversive Spirituality* (Grand Rapids, Mich.: William B. Eerdmans Pub. Co., 1997), 28.

2. E. L. Doctorow, *City of God: A Novel* (New York: Random House, 2000), 214.

3. Barbara Brown Taylor, *When God Is Silent* (Cambridge, Mass.: Cowley Publications, 1998), 107.

4. Irwin Shaw, "In Praise of the Short Story," *Esquire* 79, no. 2 (1973): 39.

5. Arthur John Gossip, *The Hero in Thy Soul* (New York: Charles Scribner's Sons, 1929), 109.

6. John Harvard's Journal, *Harvard Magazine* 83, no. 3 (1981): 61.

CHAPTER TEN

Always Tangibilitate

Unconventional religious movements have been part of the American scene almost from the beginning. Perhaps that isn't surprising, since many of the first settlers came to America seeking religious freedom; and while some of these seekers weren't unduly ready to extend such freedoms to others, the mood they established must have infected others.

Among America's religious movements, none was more remarkable than the one led by the man who came to be known as Father Divine (c. 1880–1965).[1] The work he and his wife established, first in Long Island, then Harlem, and finally in Philadelphia, eventually spread to a number of countries. Divine, an African American, gathered a following among varieties of people, probably especially among the dispossessed. He claimed twenty million followers, but biographers estimate two million would be a more accurate figure. Nevertheless, that's a remarkable number of people to accept someone's claim that he is God. On occasion, he was asked how he could amass so many followers when other preachers struggled to get a crowd. He was said to have replied, perhaps with a bit of scorn, that the other preachers didn't know how to *tangibilitate*. The word isn't in the dictionary, but the concept is clear. To make something tangible is to make it real, actual, or definite, rather than imaginary, theoretical, or vague.

To tangibilitate means several things to a preacher. Above all, perhaps, it means preaching where people live. Mitch Albom discovered a whole new world after publication of his longtime best-selling book *Tuesdays with Morrie*, a record of weekly visits with a man who was dying of Lou Gehrig's Disease. As the book became increasingly popular, Albom found that people—strangers, in the airport, on the street—would report their troubles to him. From it all, he says, "I have learned how much sadness people carry around with them."[2]

This doesn't mean that a sermon is an unceasing report on pain, because sadness isn't the only thing we carry around with us. People need a relationship with their laughter and the commonness of their days as badly as a relationship with their profound agonies. The point is, the preacher deals with real life, not with statistical studies nor abstract theories. Whether we preachers talk about sickness, death, or the Holy Trinity, we'd better find concepts and language that feel real. Our words, our gestures, our voice, the very organization of our material must have a kind of blood-and-sinew quality about them. Tangibilitate.

You may feel that I'm saying nothing other than that a preacher should be real. That's an essential beginning, but it's more than that. I've known some preachers who were very real, but they didn't tangibilitate; and on the other hand, I regret that I've known some who were (I fear) a bit phony, but they had a gift for making themselves and their material seem tangible. It is partly a gift for feeling what others feel, but if one doesn't have the gift, I think empathy can be developed.

When George M. Cohan, the legendary actor, playwright, and songwriter, was asked the secret of his success, he answered, "I'm an ordinary guy who knows what ordinary guys like to see." If this is important for the playwright, it is quintessentially more important for the preacher. What ordinary people need to hear ought to come naturally to us, because we're dealing with the most fundamental issues of human life. However, we are members of a profession, and we receive a professional education. Each day of that education, and of the professional reading we do afterwards, can remove us one more step from the people with whom we're trying to relate. Rudyard Kipling said in his poem "If—," "If you can . . . walk with Kings—nor lose the common touch, . . . you'll be a Man, my son!" I submit that if you can consort with scholars, both on paper and in person, yet talk with your congregation on Sunday morning so that they will hear you clearly and know that you belong to them—well, you're quite a preacher, my friend! Some go about it superficially, seeking to prove their commonness by an occasional bit of profanity, or a bit of questionable humor, but usually this only adds to the person's phoniness. It's a matter of remembering that we are part of the common clay, and of not being sorry about it. And especially, it is not feeling contempt for others when their commonness is painfully apparent. It is the ability to hurt with people, exult with them, laugh with them, be embarrassed with them, and then, letting this ability permeate the sermon.

It was the absence of commonness in a preacher that almost convinced Ralph Waldo Emerson never to go to church again. He recalled the experience in his famed Divinity School Address, noting that the "snow-storm [outside] was real, the preacher merely spectral. . . . He had lived in vain. He had no one word intimating that he had laughed or wept, was married or in love, had been commended, or cheated, or chagrined. If he had ever lived and acted, we were none the wiser for it. The capital secret of his profession, namely, to convert life into truth, he had not learned."[3]

However, let me say that I think none of us can achieve commonness all of the time, with all people. Cultural groups, ethnic groups, and age groups interpret reality differently, and the very quality that may help a preacher tangibilitate to a retirement community may cause him or her to turn off the twenty-something crowd. We preach now in a culture which has been cut up into more age and interest groups than would have been imaginable a decade or two ago. I think some of these differences are less distinct than imagined, but the more people accept them, the more they become distinct. And yet, some themes have a way of bridging differences. *Fiddler on the Roof* is a musical with all of its roots in Jewish life in the Western world. But when it first showed in Tokyo, a Japanese drama critic wrote in his newspaper, "How can such a foreign play be so Japanese?" Anyone who has seen *Fiddler* wants to answer, "Because it tangibilitates." Or to put it another way, because it has soul.

Let me hasten to say that I am *not* recommending that we choose our themes on the basis of what interests people. Most of us humans need to get beyond the rather selfish boundaries of our interests. The preacher ought not to cater to such self-centeredness, but rather make all subjects as interesting and as tangible as possible.

At no point is tangibilitating more crucial than when we get into matters of application and action. I was taught this lesson rather painfully one Monday morning many years ago when the church caretaker gave me an unsigned bulletin he had found in a back pew. I can't quote it exactly, but I can come close: "Dr. Kalas, we all want to be the kind of person you describe. Just tell us *how*." I've been learning from that message ever since.

Sermons are so often unfocused. They deal in grand generalities, recommendations with which no one is likely to disagree. They deal not in any real point of action, or demonstration of how to perform such an action if it has been offered. I wonder to what degree we have injured psyches by regularly holding up attractive destinations but not explaining how to get there? Sometimes, unfortunately, the answers we give to this question only accentuate our failure. On the one extreme, we slip easily into well-intentioned but lame generalities. Having faithfully diagnosed some problem, we conclude with a reminder that prayer never fails, or that we dare not lose hope. True enough, but the listener knew that before we said it. On the other extreme, we can fall into the "three wonderful rules" syndrome of the self-help magazines. Simple answers look good—good enough that they sell a lot of magazines! But examined more carefully, they're found to be as substantial and nourishing as meringue.

I surely don't mean to discredit the inspirational value of preaching. There are times when the preacher can do no greater thing than simply to lift the hearer's heart to take a new hold on life. In truth, many problems with which we human beings have to cope don't really have an answer. Many people live with circumstances as confining as any jail cell, and all of us have days, weeks, or months of this sort of confinement at some point in our lives. If the sermon gives us the heart to endure, and even to find victory in the midst of our darkness, then it has done a very, very great thing.

But the sermon that lifts the heart will still have to tangibilitate. It will need to show that the preacher knows whereof he or she speaks. The sermon will not treat the problem superficially; it will show that the preacher has had some encounters with pain. I have recalled many scores of times the summer day when Glenn Reed stopped to chat. He had wanted to preach, but no one gave him the opportunity. So now he was a bookkeeper, and found his ministry teaching Sunday school class. He had become my advocate, finding opportunities for me to preach in small-town and rural churches.

"You're going to be a fine preacher, Ellsworth," he began. "In fact, you're already better than some people who've been at it for twenty years." (I have since learned that this is not necessarily a high compliment.) "But I wouldn't want you as my pastor. You know why?"

I had been listening with full sixteen-year-old attentiveness, and I was anxious to know why. Truth is, I couldn't imagine any reason! "Because," Glenn said, "you don't have any scars. You'll be a much better preacher when you get some scars."

I've accumulated a fair number of scars since then; enough, at least, to know better than to fake them. We can't experience every human trial and tragedy, and we only prove our shallowness if in our preaching or our counseling we say too easily, "I understand. I know what you're going through." If we're dealing with such a problem in a sermon, we tangibilitate better if we say, "I've never experienced something so profound as this; I feel as if I'm walking on sacred ground when I try to discuss it. But believe me when I say that my heart wants to understand." People generally sense when we feel for them, and we had better not try to convey more than we honestly feel.

When it comes to applying a sermon, to tangibilitate means walking a careful course. On the one hand, we want to give specific suggestions when possible, so that perhaps a person can go home with some tangible possibilities in mind—but we don't want those suggestions to be pat formula. On the other hand, we want people to experience an emotional lift, whether with or without specific steps. In any event, they should know that we care.

Dr. Roy L. Smith, who was often referred to in his generation as "Mr. Methodist," said that he had learned much from an older preacher who promised him that "there is one thing of which you may be very sure. . . . Your audience will always be made up of wistful people."[4] Smith's advisor was right. Some of them keep their yearning pretty well hidden, but it's there, and the preacher needs to remember it. Those who remember will tangibilitate.

Notes

1. Daniel G. Reid, ed. *Concise Dictionary of Christianity in America* (Downers Grove, Ill.: InterVarsity Press, 1995), 359.

2. Authors Guild Foundation Symposium, "What Do I Do for an Encore?" *Authors Guild Bulletin* (Summer 2001): 24.

3. Joel Porte, " 'I am not the man you take me for': Ralph Waldo Emerson Delivers a Bombshell at the Harvard Divinity School," *Harvard Magazine* 81, no. 5 (1979): 50.

4. Roy L. Smith, *Tales I Have Told Twice* (Nashville: Abingdon Press, 1964), 87.

CHAPTER ELEVEN

The Preacher as Renaissance Person

It was my extraordinary privilege to serve as a pastor for ten years in Madison, Wisconsin, the city where earlier I had been both an undergraduate and graduate student. The privilege was all the greater in that I returned there little more than a decade after completing my bachelor's degree, so that most of my former teachers were still around—some of them even in my congregation. Among those former teachers, though not a member of my church, was the professor from whom I had taken the basic course in public speaking. We had many passing conversations during those latter years, and a surprising number of them ended with the same brief catechism.

"So you're preaching every Sunday?"

"All except four or five a year."

"You're preaching forty-seven or forty-eight times a year?"

"Right you are."

"It's not possible, you know. It isn't possible to say something interesting and worthwhile that many times a year."

I was always glad for this conversation. It reminded me of the nearly impossible nature, intellectually speaking, of the preacher's task. Taken seriously, its challenge will drive a preacher to constant study. Taken too seriously, it will drive a preacher to despair.

The truth is, those of us who serve as parish pastors have a daunting assignment. It was less daunting in those generations when the preacher was the most educated person in town, and sometimes nearly the only one. But it's quite another matter today, when in many churches a majority of the adult members are college graduates, and some have various graduate and professional degrees as well. And it's even more unnerving after a decade or two have slipped by and a pastor realizes that many in the congregation have degrees in subjects that didn't exist in his or her own college days. Therefore, preachers seek to lay hold of a role that hardly anyone else dares, but that is very appropriate for us, that of a Renaissance person.

The earliest expression of a Renaissance person may well have been unduly humanistic, with a tendency to hubris. The concept came into its own in the twentieth century, representing an admirable goal: to become a thorough, well-rounded person, someone who loves learning and who has more than a superficial knowledge of a wide variety of subjects. History's "Renaissance man" was well educated about a rather complete number of subjects. That kind of knowledge isn't possible in our day, but a modern Renaissance person knows enough things to enter into intelligent discussion with wide varieties of people—and that's what a preacher should hope to be and do. It's a quite impossible dream, of course. But nevertheless, becoming a Renaissance person is worth pursuing, because in the pursuing we will at least approach our dream. It's a dream we're obligated to pursue, because the preacher, more than any other person, is supposed to speak to all classes and conditions of persons. Other people are allowed to stay within their area of expertise. But because the area we represent involves the whole human being—body, mind, and spirit—and both time and eternity—we have to venture bravely, even if carefully, into all knowledge.

This assignment is the more difficult now because university education isn't as universal as it once was. Once, a college diploma signified an educated person; now it is more likely to signify someone who has been trained for a particular field, and more specifically, to make a living in that field. I submit that a preacher should restore the classical quality to his or her education, in order to be at home in the whole world of knowledge. I confess readily that I fall short of my goal; I'm deficient particularly in the physical sciences and the ancient classics. If I had it to do over again, I would learn enough to be able to listen intelligently. This is essentially our hope: to become intelligent listeners. And beyond that hope, to know enough that our sermons can range over a wide territory without ending in some embarrassing wilderness. This means that we will read and listen widely and selectively. We will choose our sources for both reading and listening, knowing that there may be much more misinformation awaiting us than information; this is particularly true of the Internet.

I have been privileged over the years to sit at table with some great listeners. They were all the more great because they were people who could easily have chosen to pontificate, rather than to listen. Let me mention three. Charles A. Wells used to lecture across the country, and to publish a newsletter that analyzed world events in light of the Christian faith. It was fascinating to watch him at a luncheon table, constantly seeking the opinions of those around him. Ralph W. Sockman was generally seen as the greatest preacher of his era, and Norman Vincent Peale was a genius in applying the Christian faith to the problems and possibilities of daily living. At a luncheon or dinner table, it was difficult to get them to talk about themselves; instead, they were soliciting the insights and concerns of people around them. The essayist Francis Bacon said that "conference [maketh] a ready man." We learn much by judicious listening.

We can't begin to read everything that is published; not even all that is published in our own field. We need to develop some judgment, because it takes almost as long to read junk as to read quality. John Ruskin, the nineteenth century British critic, said, "All books are divisible into two classes, the books of the hour and the books of all time." Somewhere else Ruskin reminded us that when we choose to read a given book, we are for that moment rejecting all other books in order to choose that one. This doesn't mean that we shouldn't sometimes read simply for pleasure, but it does mean that we should always read intentionally.

I am coming late to many books that I wish I had encountered earlier. But this is not all loss. I now read with greater appreciation, and with more background for context, than was the case in my youth. And believe me, I am now reading more selectively. There is some value in the "one hundred best" lists that were drawn up at the turn of the millennium. I wouldn't consider such a list sacred, but I would use it for what it's worth.

I'm glad for great periodicals. Joseph Epstein, a superb essayist, and for many years editor of *The American Scholar*, says that good periodicals may be the best source of education. To be candid, I have seen many a ten-page essay that said more than books twenty times its size. I'm grateful that my early adult years coincided with the heyday of *The Saturday Review*; I don't see anything quite like it today. Several major book review periodicals stimulate the mind, as does a quarterly journal like *The American Scholar*. Search for such journals in a public library. Find those that have a wide-ranging collection of articles, essays, poetry, and book reviews, and then look especially for the one or two that will speak to your soul. Give yourself time to process and reflect upon what you've read. Let what you read become your own, so it gets something of the imprint of your own soul.

Give proper credit when you quote something, or when you use an idea that you've taken from someone else. Always give credit. Even as you quote someone else, the hearer should sense that the material also belongs to you—not by birth, but by adoption. The major goal for the preacher is to find reading material that stimulates thinking—not just data, not just information, but ideas—until at last you find yourself pushing from the ideas you read to ideas of your own.

Preachers and laypersons who read widely in devotional literature are likely to know of A. W. Tozer. Tozer became a Christian in his midteens, and soon felt a call to preach.[1] He had only an eighth-grade education, and his family needed his financial support; it was impossible for him to go to college. That closed the door to ordination in the Methodist Church, which was then his denomination. Instead, he was ordained in 1920 by The Christian and Missionary Alliance. He set about to educate himself, and did so with a passion. When he heard that Shakespeare was essential to an educated person, he read through Shakespeare's works on his knees. Knowledge was that important to him. In time he became not only a widely known pastor, but eventually the editor of his denomination's weekly magazine and the author of some thirty books.

Such is the passion for knowledge that should drive us all. In our day of burgeoning data, no one can know everything, but the preacher should know enough to listen well and to speak intelligently. We should check our facts, lest we offend those who know more. And we should seek to become, as nearly as possible, Renaissance persons. No one has a better reason for doing so than we who approach the sacred desk.

Note

1. A. W. Tozer, *The Pursuit of God* (Harrisburg, Pa.: Christian Publications, 1982), 5-7.

CHAPTER TWELVE

With All That Is in Me

If like Oscar Hammerstein said, "a bell's not a bell till you ring it, and a song's not a song till you sing it," just as surely a sermon isn't a sermon until we preach it. I've read hundreds of sermons written by other persons, and I've written several of my own that other people tell me they have read, so I'm not about to minimize the value of words on a printed page. But something special happens when those words are delivered to us through the voice, face, eyes, carriage, and gestures of a person.

I dare say that Paul felt as much when he said, "But how are they to call on one in whom they have not believed? And how are they to believe in one of whom they have never heard? And how are they to hear without someone to proclaim him? . . . So faith comes from what is heard" (Romans 10:14, 17). I don't mean to build a doctrine around the single word *heard*; I recognize readily that the Holy Spirit uses the printed word, else I myself wouldn't try to write. Nor do I think that the hearing-impaired are in any way second-class recipients of truth. I do believe there is something that might be called "mystical" in the communication that takes place person to person. I think it is more than incidental that Paul, who realized that people said, "His letters are weighty and strong, but his bodily presence is weak, and his speech contemptible" (2 Corinthians

10:10), made his case for the hearing, not the reading, of the word.

Some recent studies in early child development give new insight on the importance of words that are personally communicated. Sandra Blakeslee of *The New York Times* news service, reported from a White House conference on early child development that "spoken language has an astonishing effect on an infant's brain development. In fact, some researchers say the number of words an infant hears each day is the single most important predictor of later intelligence, school success and social competence." But there's a catch, as Ms. Blakeslee quickly notes: "The words have to come from an attentive, engaged human being. As far as anyone has been able to determine, radio and television do not work."[1] As one who ministered via radio for over forty years, and television for a good number, I have respect for these media, and I encourage their use for preaching and teaching. But there is something special about a message delivered by a real human being who is physically present.

So why do we not give more attention to the way a sermon is delivered? One might easily feel, from reading most homiletical textbooks, that preaching is nothing but a compositional art. It seems to be assumed that if a sermon is logically developed and well written, it will succeed. I think there was a better chance of this in a time when people felt a greater loyalty to denomination and congregation; and I'm sure the sermon had a better chance when a preacher's only real competition was the colleague on the next corner, or the semiannual visit from a lecturer on tour. But brothers and sisters, you and I are in the big leagues now. Like it or not, we are somehow compared with the persons who read the six o'clock news, and the performers who appear, so well orchestrated, on the television or computer screen.

The Voice

Other generations held high opinions about the importance of the voice. Cicero said that it held "the highest place" in effective and admirable delivery. John A. Broadus, whose nineteenth century work on preaching is still sought out in this twenty-first century, said that "nothing else in a man's physical construction is nearly so important"; whatever other strengths a speaker might have, the voice was crucial.[2] In contrast, a contemporary book on preaching spends most of the little time given to the voice on discussing the use of the microphone. The microphone is important, as are the people who sit at the microphone's controls, but a microphone can't turn a poor voice into a good one, nor can it help a speaker to preserve a voice that is being misused.

So how does one get a good voice? I'm fascinated by the reasoning of two speech professors from a long generation ago, Sara Lowery and Gertrude E. Johnson. They were both specialists in interpretive reading, who taught at major universities. A good voice, they said, is needed to convey noble thoughts, and "the expression of noble thoughts in turn tends to purify the tones." If professors Lowery and Johnson were right, preachers ought to have singularly fine voices! They taught that a great voice depended, first, on an adequate instrument, and second, upon a magnetic personality. And what makes a magnetic personality? "Kindness, tolerance, appreciation, and unselfish interest in others."[3] I speak with prejudice, but if Lowery and Johnson are right, the essence of a great voice begins with soul.

Probably the most important rule in voice preservation is learning to breathe properly from the diaphragm. This means seeking out a voice teacher. It's a good investment; less expensive than throat surgery, and better than having your effective ministry cut short. And while working with a voice teacher, you will learn some vocal exercises. They stand you in good stead for opening your vocal cords as you enter a long morning of speaking. A voice teacher will probably also advise you to stay away from milk and milk products just before speaking, because they coat the throat. Some also urge limited use of caffeine products before speaking. Although you may enjoy a glass of ice water just before entering the service, you'll do better by your voice if you drink water at room temperature. As for having water in the pulpit, if you form the habit, you'll find that you have to have it—and probably, you really don't need it. Better not form the habit. It's hard to take that sip of water without its intruding.

Watch your posture! A congregation won't see the placement of your feet when you're behind a pulpit, but they'll hear it. Casual standing doesn't make for strong production, and while shouting may in its fashion make up for the lapse, it will do so at the cost of your voice. Weslea Whitfield, the ballad singer, has never forgotten the counsel of her first voice teacher, who told her that she should always "know the aria from her toes up." There's some irony in this counsel, since Miss Whitfield was shot by an assailant several years ago and left paralyzed from her hips down. But she says emotionally, she still sings from her toes up.

Begin the sermon at a conversational level. For one thing, the congregation isn't ready for more. You may shock them by a dramatic burst, but you won't advance their engagement with you. Nor is your voice ready for more. Perhaps it's fortunate that your voice and your audience are at the same place as a sermon starts. In the same fashion, it's important to have plenty of power in reserve. Don't preach at such a level that you can go no higher when the material insists on a place still higher; and of course, don't operate at such a level that the audience simply can't handle any more emphasis.

Remember that increasing volume is only one way to give emphasis, and it isn't usually the best way. I hear preachers who, in announcing the Eternal Game, show the same excitement for a one yard gain at midfield as for a 98-yard touchdown run. Variation is the secret; variation at both the level of tone and the speed of speech. Much of what one says can be delivered at the standard rate of 125 to 150 words a minute; and when one is giving rather routine material, the speed should be at the upper end. But when emphasis is desired, the speaker can slow down so that every word counts (and may they be well-chosen words!), and the voice can be either raised or lowered.

Remember that nothing takes the place of distinctness in speech. Sloppy articulation and enunciation will not be remedied by the public address system. Those who are hard of hearing don't usually need a louder preacher, but a clearer one. Certain regional speech patterns are careless of "-ing" words, so that the audience gets "preachin', thinkin', lovin', hopin', prayin'." This isn't fair treatment of a noble tongue. Be careful, too, of words that are difficult to articulate, like "shrink" or "expects." And be especially attentive to the phrases that are used so regularly that they become mumbled nothings. "Let us pray," a grand call to the greatest of all conversations, becomes in most churches "Lettuspray." The newcomer would be better off at a Latin mass, because at least he or she would know that the language was intentionally foreign.

Eye Contact

In a day when his fledgling Methodist preachers were often in danger of being pelted with old eggs or vegetables, John Wesley taught them to "always look a mob in the eye."[4] The rule is just as important when speaking to a gathering that is pleasant, affirming, and not given to untoward display. Indeed, what Wesley's preachers were compelled by fear to do, we should be compelled by love to do. After all, how else can you talk with someone except by looking at them? Take the person at the checkout counter. Some, harried by time and perhaps tired of the rejection of customers, say the customary "Have a good day," but without looking at me. In such instances, I don't feel spoken to, and certainly not communicated with. The words have been shot into the air, and like the poet's arrow, where they'll land, I have no idea. Certainly not with me, because they aren't directed at me. They're directed at some mythical creature, some generality. But I'm an individual, not a generality, so I want to be looked at.

I was told in high school public speaking and debate courses always to maintain eye contact, and the rule made sense to me. But it was only a few years ago that I finally realized why the speaker's eye contact is so crucial. If you and I are in a conversation, you don't mind if I look away occasionally while I'm talking. But you don't want my eyes wandering when *you're* talking. Few things are more insulting. When I'm preaching, the congregation needs to know that I'm also listening. That's what we mean when we refer to preaching as communication; communication happens only when there's give and take. The only way the congregation knows that the preacher is listening is if the preacher looks at them. If the preacher looks over the heads, or out into space, he or she may be talking, but the congregation knows that the preacher is not listening. Whether or not the hearers analyze the scene, they instinctively know what's going on.

If the preacher has soul, the eyes do much to communicate it. The eyes of the speaker are not very visible when the meeting place seats several hundred or more, but the intent of the speaker is. If the speaker really cares about the persons being spoken to, he or she will look at them, in order to see what they are saying. Their body language may upset us: "I'm bored." "Next week is going to be tough." "I hope we get to brunch on time." But I need to hear these things, need to hear them as much as that kind person who is saying, "I love every word you say." I prefer the latter, of course, but I need very much to hear the former—and if possible, do something helpful about it.

Gestures

When Demosthenes was asked about the first, second, and third *desiderata* of rhetoric, he answered, "Action, action, action." I'm sure he didn't have in mind the speaker who strides ceaselessly across the platform, but he may well have had in mind the many instruments with which a speaker can communicate besides voice and words: eyes, eyebrows, head, hands, arms, torso, and mouth. Popular psychology teaches us a great deal about body language and the degree to which it influences us. I doubt, however, that even the best testing methodology can really measure the degree to which we are persuaded or repelled, charmed or repulsed, by the intangibles of body language.

Lydia Masterkova, the Russian artist of the twentieth century, had something bordering on disdain for language. In Paris, she would see many movies without knowing the language on the sound track; then, talking with persons who had seen the same films and understood the dialogue, she insisted that they had often missed some of the most important details. She insisted that "the word is a signal that limits the horizon and breaks the continuity of thought."[5] Even if Masterkova was overstating the point, as many of us would feel, we need still to understand what she is saying. The eyes of the listener pick up all sorts of communication from our hands, our body, our posture. I suspect that Masterkova would have subscribed to the story that, on an occasion when Saint Francis was too ill to preach, he simply stood mute before his congregation, and "gazed on them with love."

The preacher's body messages begin quite some time before the sermon. If the worship time includes a processional, the preacher says something by the style of entrance. Does he or she look distracted? Is he or she not singing? Is his or her carriage naturally erect, or is it self-consciously pompous? Or is it, on the other hand, carelessly slouching to Bethlehem? Even in a less formal service, the preacher's entrance is equally an object of attention and of impression. We have begun to preach without having said a word, and so it continues, through our posture on the platform or chancel, our attentiveness to others who participate in the service, and our indication of either involvement or preoccupation.

Our body language comes to full flower (or unseemly weed, perhaps) as we preach. For one thing, gestures should be consistent with the content. I sometimes see preachers gesturing vigorously during material that is pure data, just the conveying of information. Most sermons include an amount of such material; it is valuable, but not in the fashion that calls for extravagant movement. So, too, some types of material call for solemnity in gesturing, while another kind makes exuberance the mood. All of this is really a matter of common sense, but one has to conclude, in observing much preaching, that common sense isn't all that common.

Naturalness is crucial in good gesturing. One reason it's so difficult to teach gesturing for the pulpit is that gestures ought to flow unbidden from the speaker. True gestures precede the words, although only by a spilt second; it seems to be the way our motor system is hooked up. If we "learn" to gesture, an unconscious artificiality will surface. I repeat: we are communicators, not actors or performers. A staginess that is acceptable for a performer arouses skepticism when used by a preacher.

The degree to which gestures are a matter of soul is demonstrated by the tie between gestures and language.

When the legendary Fiorello La Guardia was mayor of New York, he campaigned easily in English, Italian, and Yiddish, which gave him a great advantage with those large language segments of the Gotham population. Veteran observers said that they could tell which language was being used simply by watching La Guardia's gestures. I remember viewing tapes by a seminary candidate who was preaching to a mixed audience in English and Spanish. As he alternated from paragraph to paragraph, I marveled at how the gestures changed between languages, even though the written content was nearly identical.

Gestures should almost always be suggestive rather than imitative. Only occasionally should a preacher try to portray an action. Billy Sunday could slide into home plate during a sermon, because it was consistent with his persona and with what the audience expected of him. But most of us had better stay with just enough gesture to elicit the viewer's imagination. Imitative gestures can easily give a preacher the quality of a buffoon; laughter is acceptable if that is the preacher's goal, but laughter sometimes comes at a high price. As for highly dramatic enactments, the preacher had better be well trained in drama, else those observing will be in pain other than the cathartic pain the speaker intended.

The pulpit is an impediment to gestures, especially if one is shorter and the pulpit is unnecessarily high. If you're there for more than one stop, better get a raised platform! But in any event, the preacher needs to get high enough for his or her arms to be seen; what happens out of the viewer's sight level edifies no one.

Gestures have planes of domain. At the midchest level, gestures signify the human and the humane. This is the area of most "normal" gesturing, the gestures that help communicate the explanatory portions of the sermon and that give emphasis and clarity to the unfolding of ideas. The area of the shoulders and head signify the noble, the intellectual, the higher ground of life. Hands extended over the head speak of the profoundly spiritual and the heavenly. Woe to the preacher who berates the sins of the flesh with hands raised high, or who speaks of the beauty and nobility of life with hands hanging dumbly at the sides.

And remember that almost always, two hands are better than one. A lone hand can hardly help but be didactic at best, and accusing at worst. Two hands, however, are embracing. Speak a sentence with one hand extended and the finger pointing, and the audience knows it is being told what to do; speak the same words with both arms extended and the audience feels it is being invited to enter the challenge with you.

A sincere smile is one of the best of gestures. It dare not be phony or practiced; it must come from your soul, and from your genuine affection for people. An honest smile, like a spoonful of sugar, helps the medicine go down. A smile is especially important early in a sermon, unless the subject matter absolutely forbids it. When you smile, listeners marry your message. And if you're lucky, they won't divorce your message for the rest of the sermon, even though your sermon may sometimes not be fit to live with.

Gestures almost never lie. I suspect that people know this instinctively, so they believe our gestures more than our words. If I say, "Come unto me, all you that labor and are heavy-laden" while my hands lie at my side, the hearer will sense that I don't really mean it. Many a preacher has exhorted a congregation that they must begin loving one another, but they've seen his clenched fists, and have gotten the angry and frustrated signal of his gestures rather than the message of his words.

When I sense during a sermon that a particular gesture is dominating my action, I ask myself what is going on in my soul. If my open hand shapes into a continually clenched fist, something is happening inside me. If my hands get into a frequent pattern of circular movement, I'm almost surely struggling to get my thoughts organized, or to find better words for the insight. If my animation is markedly low, it's a signal that I'm physically tired, or perhaps not as taken by this gathering of people as I ought to be. In any event, these gestures (or lack thereof) reveal what is going on in my soul, and I seek—even as I speak—for inner healing. When everything is right, the voice seems full and easy of production, it's impossible not to have eye contact because you want so much to talk with these people, and the gestures flow so naturally that you might well be Cicero. At such times, preaching is very heavenly. And at such times you pray that you will never again preach any other way.

Notes

1. Sandra Blakeslee, "Babies, It Seems, Are Wired for Mental Success," *The Lexington Herald-Leader* (18 April 1997): A-1.

2. John A. Broadus, *On the Preparation and Delivery of Sermons*, rev. ed. (New York: Harper and Brothers, 1944), 339.

3. Sara Lowrey and Gertrude E. Johnson, *Interpretative Reading: Techniques and Selections* (New York: D. Appleton-Century Company, 1942), 180.

4. Halford E. Luccock and Paul Hutchinson, *The Story of Methodism* (Nashville: Abingdon-Cokesbury Press, 1926), 94.

5. Anthony Astrackan, "Alone Abroad: Soviet Artists in Exile," *The Atlantic Monthly* 243, no. 2 (1979): 75.

CHAPTER THIRTEEN
The Importance of Being Imperfect

There's no catch in this title. I really mean that imperfection is important. You may well judge that there's no need for you to read this chapter, because imperfection is one of your strong points. If so, I want to help you understand that imperfection has its place in preaching, and help you learn how to use it effectively.

My sympathy with imperfection is consistent with my philosophy of soul preaching. Soul preaching is, by definition, an imperfect instrument. Anything that is delivered from a human soul will have all sorts of smudges and irregularities. Some people are disturbed by what they perceive to be errors in the Bible, or at the least, matters that don't appeal to them. Not I. I see the Bible as a soul book, a book that has come from the Person of God, but that has traveled through the souls of those who have delivered it to us. I expect, therefore, that it will bear the marks of these human agents. How could it be otherwise?

Someone has said that there is no beauty without a blemish. I think that also means that the blemish is part of the beauty. And surely it is never more true than when we're speaking of preaching. I consider preaching an art, but it is never as neat and polished as a painting, a poem, a symphony, or a play. We may look at a painting and feel that not a brush stroke is wasted, or plead that not a note be dropped from a classic symphony. Not so with a sermon. A sermon is not complete on paper, where it might seek unblemished beauty; a sermon becomes a sermon when a preacher delivers it and hearers receive it. In that delivery process—the soul process itself—imperfections appear. It can't be otherwise, because the sermon ebbs and flows with its hearers, and that rhythm is inevitably irregular. Yet, strangely enough, this is where a sermon gets its consummate beauty. No sermon on paper, even if that were a fair medium for judgment, can be compared with a sermon delivered with passion and received with grace. Walter Russell Bowie was probably one of the most polished pulpiteers of his time, but he called for the "stirrings of the spirit which are more sovereign than rules which homiletic formalists may lay down."[1]

Seek Excellence

Now let me be very clear. I am not suggesting, even remotely, that we should be content with mediocrity because we embrace imperfection. Such an idea is blasphemous. Nor ought we to console our infirmities by noting the weaknesses in well-known preachers. In truth, some of the most obvious failings exist in some of the most popular preachers; they become known and loved for some distortion that in another preacher, is condemned.

This may be a particular hazard for the soul preacher. In the process of becoming ourselves and of delivering our own souls, we may become something of a character, so that people love us for our peculiarities. These personal characteristics become charming, and a preacher can come to use them—indeed, to exploit them. If we do, we become less a preacher—a conveyor of truth—and more a personality, a performer. We may become like those movie personalities who always play themselves, and that's bad news for a preacher, since a preacher shouldn't do too much business with the self.

We should strive mightily for excellence—not perfection, but excellence. Students of medieval architecture remind us that the stonemasons who produced intricate figures scores of feet above the street and out of any normal view chose to develop them in such detail because they believed God would see their work. Such should be our passion.

I find it interesting that the case for imperfection isn't limited to the preaching enterprise. Jorie Graham scrutinizes her final draft of a poem against her first draft to guard against "the arc of emotion" being "prettified," or having "the wind knocked out of it by writerly technique, by 'good writing.' "[2] Why would a poet be worried about "good writing"? Poetry must have soul or it has nothing at all. If, as William Wordsworth said, poetry is "the spontaneous overflow of powerful feelings," there will be some irregularity in it. With all of its attention to meter and sometimes to rhyme, poetry will nevertheless have some untamed quality. So, too, with really fine acting. Jack Lemmon was already a rather fine actor by the time he first came under the direction of George Cukor. After each of Lemmon's speeches in rehearsal, Cukor would cry, "Less, less, less!" Lemmon finally asked, "Don't you want me to act at all?" To which Cukor replied, "Dear boy, you're beginning to understand."

For the preacher, the danger of skill was probably said best by that most incisive critic of human nature, Holden Caulfield, in *The Catcher in the Rye*: "If you do something *too* good, then, after a while, if you don't watch it, you start showing off."[3] This is the mood, at its extreme, that Thomas Hardy describes so bitingly in his poem, "In Church": the preacher whose "voice thrills up to the topmost tiles," and who then, in the supposed privacy of his vestry reenacts it all "in deft dumb-show," and "with a satisfied smile."[4] The preacher who becomes too practiced, too flawless, is likely to become more an actor than a proclaimer. This is a problem for certain elements of delivery; one can perfect a gesture for a stage play, but I doubt one can for a sermon, a rehearsed vocal emphasis, or any trick of timing that is stagy. The preacher is not a performer, but a messenger. The preacher must never succumb to manipulating an audience. People are to be reasoned with, appealed to, loved, but never used. The great preacher is a great lover, and for that reason is never a polished performer. Since love is an overflow of the soul, it cannot be nicely contained or packaged. There will always be some ineptness in it, some dust and sweat.

A reporter in a large southern city wrote an article about a pastor in a major church that his congregation admitted wasn't a particularly strong preacher. The reporter noted how hard the pastor worked at his preaching: typically twenty hours of preparation, with the writing finished by Wednesday. Then he hid himself in the empty sanctuary on Wednesday night to practice his delivery, and practiced again on Thursday, Friday, and Saturday, and once more early on Sunday morning. As I read the report, I pondered the times I had heard him preach; he did, indeed, sound practiced. He needed terribly to forget his sermon, forget technique, and to simply *talk* to his people. Ironically, the man is a strong communicator in person. But he's not practiced in person; he simply tries to tell you what's on his mind. Too bad he doesn't do the same in the pulpit.

An Incompleteness Within

Edward W. Bauman, for many years pastor of a major pulpit in the nation's capital, once spoke of his "deep-seated emotional need to be liked."[5] I consider it an honorable confession. I suspect that there has never been a truly moving communicator who wasn't possessed in a substantial way of the need to be liked. At an elemental level, it is related to the entertainer's love of applause. As a result, this need is fraught with peril. When the preacher wants too much to be liked, he or she may seek affirmation at the price of integrity. Nevertheless, this deep-seated need compels the preacher to reach out in ways that show a wholesome vulnerability. It is the preacher's Paul-like thorn in the flesh. A perfectly balanced personality is rather too perfect to speak to imperfect people. The preacher might well wish to be rid of this weakness, yet to be rid of it is also to lose a peculiar source of strength. Paul said of his thorn that through it God's power was "made perfect" in his weakness. The desire for approval isn't a noble trait; I refer to it with embarrassment. But I'd be a poorer preacher if it were taken from me.

One of my students, Dale Capron, reminded me that in J. R. R. Tolkien's *The Lord of the Rings* we learn that sheep graze on fields after battles are fought there. So with the preacher's soul. Capron feels it is "this very imperfection" that makes the message so appealing to so many people. We will never preach the perfect sermon—not in the sense of a perfect symphony or an unblemished sonnet. But perfect, in a peculiar way—in the earnest, fumbling union of soul with soul. The edges of such a union will always be rough and irregular, but they will also be beautiful in ways that perfection can never be.

Notes

1. Walter Russell Bowie, *Learning to Live* (Nashville: Abingdon Press, 1969), 160.

2. Craig Lambert, "Image and the Arc of Feeling," *Harvard Magazine* 103, no. 3 (2001): 43.

3. J. D. Salinger, *The Catcher in the Rye* (New York: Little Brown, 1962), 115.

4. Louis Untermeyer, ed. *Modern British Poetry* (New York: Harcourt, Brace & World, 1942), 29.

5. Edward W. Bauman, *God's Presence in My Life* (Nashville: Abingdon Press, 1981): 76.

CHAPTER FOURTEEN

You Can't Win Them All

I watch college basketball games with amazement. Let a player commit a foolish foul or throw an errant pass, and the coach is, quite literally, in his face. Thousands in the stands and millions on television can watch while a player is scourged to humiliation. The scene in gymnastic events in the Olympics is even more unnerving. A sprite of a performer dashes to the sidelines after doing things that we ordinary mortals know are impossible; however, her coach says otherwise, impatiently and vehemently.

I'm a coach, too. I teach preaching. And sometimes I wonder what would happen if I, or any of my colleagues in homiletics, were to confront a preaching student with anything like the directness of an athletic coach. As a matter of fact, I've sometimes been told by athletes-turned-preachers that they are amazed at their vulnerability as preachers compared to their hardiness as athletes.

Are we preachers simply wimps? Perhaps, but I think some special factors are involved. One of these we share with other creative workers. Many artists have observed that if they receive a dozen enthusiastic reviews and one negative one, it's the one bad review that stays in his or her mind for days afterward. The late Sydney Harris once observed in his syndicated column that on the previous day his agent had advised him that two major papers were now taking up his column, and that a relatively minor paper had canceled. Harris found that he couldn't rejoice in the major victories for his distress in the one minor rejection.

I know the feeling. It's the price of creative ownership. The sermon is not just a job, it's a piece of one's soul. The preacher's feeling is likely to be a bit more complicated than that of other artists; it's the God thing. If the sermon has been born and developed in prayer, and if the preacher intends it to be, as much as a human dares, a word from God, he or she may easily forget how human are the hands that have delivered it. In the process of taking our task seriously, we may take ourselves too seriously. We're told that Roman conquerors had a whispering servant to remind them that all the glory of their office was temporary. We need something like that. One way or another, we need to be reminded that the attention people pay us is in truth derivative, very transient, and we have no business taking it at face value. Nor dare we accept any accolades without turning the glory to God.

But still, there's pain in the job. One is tempted, at times, to the mood of Oscar Wilde. Arriving at his club after the first performance of his play *Lady Windermere's Fan*, he was asked, "Oscar, how did your play go tonight?" "Oh," Wilde replied, "The play was a great success, but the audience was a total failure." They sometimes seem so. One Sunday morning you feel you've delivered your soul; you're not ordinarily in awe of yourself, but this sermon seemed special from its conception, through its hard labor, and into its impassioned delivery. The result? "Such a nice talk this morning, Reverend." And perhaps, "Did you intentionally leave out the announcement about our group meeting?"

That's one side of it, and I don't have to tell you how painful it is. On the other hand, you wonder some days how far you're falling short of your high calling. Could it be, some Sundays, that "The hungry sheep look up, and are not fed?" In his novel *The Spire*, William Golding mentions a period when three days of rain delayed the building of a grand church, casting a pall over the entire endeavor. Golding sums it this way: "As for the whole building itself, the bible in stone, it sank from glorification to homiletics."[1] That's an unkind word for those of us whose art is homiletics. We'd like to think that our sermons, like Ruskin's perfect architecture, are built to stand forever. But a sermon is an every-week creation; as such, it's in danger of being forgotten before next week's edition comes around. Sometimes even the preacher forgets after a week or two; this darling child, about which any criticism once seemed a mortal blow is, in ten days, homiletical dust.

Yet, there's always the chance—indeed, the pious expectation—that the sermon will live on. It may not be remembered in outline form, its title may become a jumble, and its basic idea may eventually intermarry with several less-noble lines. But we hope it will take lodging somewhere in the person's soul, and that it will someday—perhaps several times—reappear, to challenge, to comfort, and to renew. After all, Jesus said that even in those cities where the disciples would shake the dust off their feet it could still be said that the kingdom of God had come near.

Let me say what is for me a daring thing: I think that every sermon ought in some way to be Christ's Second Coming. I came to this conviction after hearing a visiting bishop preach. His sermons were true enough, well structured, and relatively sound in logic. But they didn't catch me, didn't set a fire in my soul, and that's what a sermon ought to do. It ought to be Christ coming again, sometimes quietly as when he entered a room and the disciples didn't know whence he had come, and sometimes dramatically, as in the clouds of the sky, with the shout of the archangel and the trump of God. And sometimes as he came very simply, meeting our need as when he broke bread for the disciples, cooking a meal for them at the seashore. Somehow we ought to know in the preaching of the Word, that Christ, the eternal Word, has come—even to those who do not recognize him or do not want him.

Frederick Buechner says that preaching is to "proclaim a Mystery before which, before whom, even our most exalted ideas turn to straw,"[2] and to that I say Amen. But if this is going to be delivered through the medium of my soul, I had better make that soul as good, as real, as authentic, and as utterly holy as it possibly can be. And even then, even at my soul's best, I will sometimes color the message very badly. But even then, I know two things. For one, that sometimes it is the very inappropriateness of my coloring that will, ironically, make the ineffable Word more accessible to some soul. I know that the Holy Spirit is wonderfully adept at giving adequacy to the inadequate, and at reaching quite unlikely people.

I have been preaching for a long time, and I am still unhappy with the way I do it. I have never really doubted my call, but only in my more inane moments have I thought I was fulfilling it. An alcoholic once explained his predicament to me vividly. "Reverend, I'm all right as long as things are normal, but damn it, they're never normal." Likewise, under ideal circumstances I would offer great sermons, but I never get to preach under ideal circumstances.

But I keep trying. And I keep reminding myself that you can't win them all. I want you to remember that. I keep forgetting, but I want you to remember. You can't win them all.

Notes

1. William Golding, *The Spire* (New York: Pocket Books, 1966), 43.

2. Frederick Beuchner, *Telling Secrets* (San Francisco: HarperSanFrancisco, 1991), 61.